It Happened In Missouri

It Happened In Series

It Happened In Missouri

Remarkable Events That Shaped History

Second Edition

Sean McLachlan

Guilford, Connecticut

To buy books in quantity for corporate use
or incentives, call **(800) 962-0973**
or e-mail **premiums@GlobePequot.com**.

Map by M. A. Dubé © Morris Book Publishing, LLC
Layout: Sue Murray
Project editor: Lauren Szalkiewicz

ISBN 978-0-7627-7193-6

Printed in the United States of America

10 9 8 7 6 5 4 3 2 1

The Library of Congress has previously catalogued an earlier edition as follows:

McLachlan, Sean.
 It happened in Missouri : thirty true tales from the Show-Me State / Sean McLachlan.—1st ed.
      p. cm.—(It happened in series)
  ISBN-13: 978-0-7627-4333-9
  1. Missouri—History—Anecdotes. 2. Missouri—Biography—Anecdotes. 3. Missouri—History, Local—Anecdotes. I. Title.
  F466.6.M38 2007
  977.8—dc22

                                                    2007042321

For Almudena, my wife,
and Julián, my son

CONTENTS

CONTENTS

INTRODUCTION

If you look at a map of the continental United States, you'll find Missouri right in the center. It's been at the center of a lot of the country's history as well. The confluence of the Mississippi and Missouri Rivers made the region important even in prehistoric times, when the most advanced Native American civilization in North America called it home. From the seventeenth century it became a French territory, then a Spanish one, and then briefly returned to French rule again. In 1803 Napoleon sold it to the United States as part of a vast tract of land known as the Louisiana Purchase, which doubled the size of the United States. Meriwether Lewis and William Clark, heading the Corps of Discovery, departed from St. Louis on their journey to the Pacific, and Missouri became the main path west for many pioneers. Both the Santa Fe and Oregon Trails started in Missouri.

But people didn't just pass through; Missouri's central location and economic potential meant that a wide variety of people settled here—French Canadian trappers and members of old Southern families, German immigrants fresh from Europe and Mexican traders riding up the Santa Fe Trail, adventurers and farmers, explorers and outlaws. Missouri's acceptance as a state in 1821 was the greatest event the country saw that decade, and Missouri became a crucial player in the developing Civil War. The state has more peaceful stories to tell, too, and in this book you'll find only a fraction of the many events in its colorful history.

Here are thirty-two tales of Missourians, great and small, who made contributions or added to the state's exciting lore. I won't give away how they end, but once you've read them, you'll notice many of the men and women in these pages did not live to see their goals accomplished. This is often the way with history; many of the people who make it go unrecognized or unrewarded in their lifetime, but their contributions are not forgotten.

Missouri is lucky to have two major historical societies to record and teach the state's heritage: the State Historical Society of Missouri in Columbia and the Missouri Historical Society in St. Louis. Equally important are the many local historical and genealogical societies that are carefully preserving the history of their county, town, and local families for future generations. Once you've read this book, I hope you'll look up one of these organizations, because you'll discover an endless number of stories like those collected here. Perhaps your family has some stories of its own that should be recorded while the older members are still around to tell them. While historians tend to focus on great deeds and famous names, it's really the everyday people who make the most history, and their stories are just as important as the famous inventors, musicians, and generals.

The work of many researchers, both professionals and dedicated amateurs, has gone into this book. I would especially like to thank the staff of the State Historical Society of Missouri in Columbia for helping me sift through their vast collection of newspapers, books, and journals and for their patience in answering what must have seemed like an unending stream of questions. I would also like to thank Civil War specialist Carolyn Bartels for input on the Civil War chapters, and Chris and Caitlin Davis for providing a place of refuge for a wandering writer. A very special thank-you goes out to my wife Almudena and my son Julián, for putting up with my disappearing for long periods of time into a pile of notes and papers. This book is dedicated to them.

MOUND CITY, THE CITY BEFORE ST. LOUIS

1200

In the nineteenth century, St. Louis faced a mystery. Strange mounds dotted the countryside around the small city, some only the size of a house, while others towered over the landscape. There were so many that locals often referred to St. Louis as "Mound City." Nobody knew who had built the mounds or why. Antiquarians, the predecessors of today's archaeologists, puzzled over these silent monuments from the past and worried that the rapidly expanding city would demolish all trace of them before they could solve the enigma. It seemed as though every year another mound disappeared to make way for a road or a house.

An early map of St. Louis showed several rectangular, flat-topped mounds encircling an open area like a plaza, while a line of mounds trailed away from them to the south. Farther north stood what locals called the "Big Mound," a huge circular heap of earth thirty feet high. Similar mounds existed across much of the state, especially along streams and rivers. Across the Mississippi River at Cahokia,

Illinois, near modern East St. Louis, stood a massive site with more than a hundred mounds. Worried the St. Louis mounds would soon disappear, antiquarians excavated them and discovered that most contained burials. The dead had obviously been important members of society, considering the large number of arrowheads, shell beads, and other artifacts buried with them.

In 1869, when workers planned to destroy the Big Mound to make way for a new road, antiquarians rushed to excavate it. They hoped the largest mound in the area would house the richest burials. They were not disappointed. Inside they found numerous artifacts, including conch shells, bone tools, and a strange copper ear ornament, depicting a face with a long, flat nose. Antiquarians uncovered similar objects elsewhere, and they eventually dubbed the figure "the long-nosed god." The style of the artifacts and art from mounds in other states, featuring hands, weeping eyes, snakes, suns, and birds, suggested the mounds had been the product of one great civilization. Ceramic vessels sculpted in the shape of humans or animals may have been totems for particular clans.

Early researchers dubbed this culture the "Mound Builders" and believed they had been a race of advanced people unrelated to the American Indians. Some claimed the Mound Builders were one of the Lost Tribes of Israel, or prehistoric immigrants from Europe, or an extinct people wiped out by Indian "savages." They refused to see the similarities between Indian and Mound Builder artifacts and never bothered to listen to Indian legends recording how their ancestors had built the mounds. To most academics of the time, building the mounds would have been too complicated for the Indians, whom whites generally regarded as inferior.

Archaeologists now know the mounds had been built by a number of independent groups, not a single kingdom, and they call the culture the "Mississippian" because it centered along the Mississippi, especially at Cahokia and Mound City.

Mound City's many artificial hills reflect its past glory, which was at its height around AD 1200, when the city had a thriving population numbering well over ten thousand. Unfortunately, Mound City suffered as a result of its useful location at the best place to dock a boat near where the two rivers meet—the modern river port of St. Louis grew right on top of it. The city of Cahokia, just across the river in Illinois, gives more clues as to what Mound City must have been like. The site is famous for its well-preserved mounds and fascinating Woodhenge, a ring of posts marking the rising and setting of the sun at the turn of the seasons. Researchers have estimated that by the year 1200 Cahokia had a population of about twenty thousand.

Around that time, when larger towns acted as commercial and government centers for surrounding villages, Mound City may have ruled over villages up to fifty miles away. In fact, archaeologists know of more than a dozen large towns across the southeastern part of the state, each associated with smaller communities surrounding them. One of those large towns grew up near present-day Kansas City.

While many of the mounds contained burials, others served as bases for important houses or temples. A flat-topped mound with a temple on top dominated the center of many towns. Nearby would be a mound topped by a large house for the chieftain. Commoners lived on the level earth, in houses made of a lattice of wood covered with thatch and hides.

Cahokia, Mound City, and many other towns featured open plazas surrounded by mounds, much like the ancient cities in Central America, suggesting the Mississippian culture borrowed ideas from the powerful civilizations to the south. While the two centers of civilization seem far apart, the Mississippi River offered quick travel for most of the distance, and similarities in artistic styles indicate that intrepid traders made the journey regularly.

Salt Springs near Mound City provided an important export, since many inland people didn't have access to salt. The Mississippian people also exported the beautiful products of their expert craftspeople. In exchange they imported obsidian and grizzly bear teeth from the Great Plains, shells from the Gulf Coast, copper from the Great Lakes, and other things they couldn't find locally.

However, many questions still puzzled the excavators of the Big Mound, mainly why the settlement had disappeared. It appears that towns and villages began to build defenses, suggesting they feared attack, and this uncertainty seems to have led to diminishing trade with faraway places. But while archaeology has uncovered a great deal of information about how this civilization lived, it hasn't solved the mystery of why it died.

As Mound City and other great centers along the Mississippi declined, the Oneota, a village-based tribal culture, emerged in its place. The Oneota were probably the predecessors to the historic Osage and Missouri tribes. By the time the first French missionaries arrived in the area in the 1600s, the Mississippian culture had faded into legend, but the historic tribes of Missouri can trace their lineage back to the greatest prehistoric civilization in North America.

Of all the many mounds that made up the skyline of Mound City, only one survives. At the northern end of Ohio Avenue stands a small, flat-topped mound that may have been the base for the house of an important person. A modern house shares the property, and the fact that it's in the yard of a private home explains why it wasn't destroyed along with all the others. The early excavators in St. Louis made a valiant attempt to find out about the ancient monuments before they disappeared, but their efforts were only partly successful in the face of unbridled expansion.

THE TEENAGER WHO BUILT A CITY

1764

Fourteen-year-old Auguste Chouteau examined the progress of his workers as they cleared the land and built cabins on the bluff overlooking the Missouri and Mississippi Rivers. He breathed in the fresh February air, still cold with winter and tinged by the sharp smell of campfires, and felt a sense of pride. These were his men, put under his command by his stepfather, M. Laclède Ligueste.

But he felt worried, too. His stepfather was more than a week away at Fort de Chartres, and his mother and the rest of his family were more than a month's sailing downriver in New Orleans. He was without his family for the first time in his life, in command of a group of thirty older men and given an overwhelming responsibility—to carve out a settlement in the unspoiled and remote wilderness of France's Upper Louisiana territory.

He and his stepfather had sailed up the Mississippi from New Orleans under the auspices of a new trading company owned by Laclède and partner Antoine Maxent, a wealthy New Orleans businessman. They had won exclusive trading rights with all Indian tribes west of the Mississippi for eight years, yielding a potential fortune in furs.

But Chouteau had problems from the beginning. Fort de Chartres was due to be handed over to the English soon. France had lost a war with England, and part of its punishment was to give up its lands east of the Mississippi. All of the company's goods would have to be moved out. Even worse, some of the tribes on the east bank, who had fought alongside the French against the English, vowed to continue the war. Chouteau needed to get the new town built and everything set up before the Indians made good their threat to turn the area into a war zone again.

So in February 1764 his stepfather sent him here to erect a town as quickly as possible before the expedition became homeless in the wilderness.

Chouteau built a storage shed and several cabins, and when Laclède arrived in early April, he proudly showed his stepfather around the little settlement. The older man named the place St. Louis, after King Louis IX, a famous medieval French king. Laclède chose a spot for his house, which would also serve as a trading post, and laid out plans for the village. French settlers began to arrive. They preferred to remain under French rule on the west bank of the river, fearing what would happen when the east bank came under the jurisdiction of their longtime enemies. Among these settlers were a few boys of Chouteau's age—Gregoire Kiercereau, who came with his church cantor father to mark out a spot for a church and graveyard, and Louis and Joseph Chancellor, who apparently came unaccompanied. Another family set up the town's first mill at a little stream nearby. Seeing all was going according to plan, Laclède returned to Fort de Chartres to retrieve the trade goods.

Shortly after his stepfather left, Chouteau was startled by the appearance of hundreds of Missouri Indians paddling down the Missouri River in canoes. The group included about 150 warriors, daubed in war paint and carrying knives, bows, and war clubs, but he was relieved to see the warriors had brought their families along—this was no invasion.

Once ashore, the chiefs told Chouteau they had quarreled with the Osage, a fierce tribe with whom they usually had good relations. Fearing a fight, the smaller Missouri tribe had come here, only to find a white town on their land. When Chouteau told them the French didn't mean to intrude but were instead setting up a trading post, the Indians declared that they would set up their village right next to it.

The frontier, however, was rife with tales of Indian raids on white settlers, and the tribe vastly outnumbered the tiny French settlement. Fearing the worst, most of the settlers fled back to the east bank of the Mississippi, preferring to take their chances with the English. Chouteau and his thirty men found themselves alone with no guarantee that the Missouri would stay friendly as the tribe adjusted to coexisting with settlers. Soon the Missouri demanded gifts. The Indians had a tradition of giving gifts as a sign of friendship, and if the white men wanted to settle on their land and trade with them, what would be more natural than to give the tribe some gifts?

But most of the trade goods were still in Fort de Chartres. Chouteau immediately sent word to his stepfather to hurry back to St. Louis, but he had to keep the Indians happy for a couple of weeks before Laclède arrived. Chouteau ordered his sentries to keep a sharp eye out for the Osage and kept the Missouri busy by hiring the women and children to dig out a large cellar for the house and trading post. The Indians eagerly joined in the work in exchange for metal awls as well as vermilion and verdigris, which they used for paint. The Indians liked the well-made awls, and soon other tools started disappearing from the worksite. The French workers complained that this was theft, but the Indians paid little heed. In their minds it was a form of frontier taxation.

To Chouteau's vast relief, his stepfather finally arrived with the trade goods. He handed out a great many gifts, thus securing peace with the tribe and the promise of trade in the future. The Missouri soon left St. Louis and went down to Fort de Chartres, where they convinced the commander to make peace for them with the Osage.

When Laclède visited St. Louis again in late July, Chouteau had built more of the village and was finishing up the stone trading post. Laclède also escorted the civilians from near the fort. The settlers brought all their worldly goods, even the doors and windows from their houses, and set to work building their new homes and expanding the town.

The newcomers were pleased to find many houses already built and waiting for them to move in, thanks to the efficient management of Auguste Chouteau. Among the new arrivals came the area's first free black family, known only as Gregoire and Janette. In the fall of 1764, Chouteau was delighted when his mother and his four younger siblings arrived. He still had plenty of responsibilities, but at least he was no longer alone.

St. Louis soon blossomed into a thriving trading post. The Missouri and Osage, at peace again, arrived in canoes piled with furs to trade with the French, and many of the settlers went off to trap furs themselves. The village at the confluence of the Missouri and Mississippi Rivers soon became the largest French settlement west of the Mississippi and would continue to be so for many years. Chouteau, who had already proved himself a man, grew up to be one of the most influential leaders in the territory, even after it became part of the United States. His leadership skills and quick thinking beyond his years had earned him the respect of the rough frontier society.

THE BATTLE OF FORT SAN CARLOS

1780

The citizens of St. Louis, in the Spanish province of Louisiana, feared for their lives. As townsfolk carried water from nearby wells, tilled the fields, and hewed logs for their cabins, they exchanged nervous rumors that the British had dispatched an army to burn and plunder the thriving settlement. The rumors had a basis in fact—they came from reports by spies and friendly Indians who had come to warn the local Spanish lieutenant governor, Captain Fernando de Leyba.

American settlements on the east bank of the Mississippi had favored the cause of independence and rebelled against British control. Both the Americans and the British saw the river as a potential supply route for sneaking arms and munitions around the navies stationed on the East Coast. France and Spain openly sided with the American colonists because the rebellion hurt their common enemy, the British Empire.

The British government had organized the Indians in the Michigan area, including the Sac, Fox, Winnebago, Sioux, and other tribes, and promised them that if they invaded the Spanish territory and captured St. Louis, they could ransack the town and every farm they came across. To European civilians willing to fight, the government offered trading rights on the Missouri River, something the Spanish had denied them.

One of these civilians was Emanuel Hesse, a hunter who knew the area well. He led an army of approximately 750 men, mostly Indians along with some civilians and a few British soldiers. Although this army seems small by modern standards, it outnumbered the entire population of St. Louis at the time.

Back in St. Louis, Leyba hurriedly organized a defense. He was seriously ill, so weak that he couldn't walk or even write a letter, but he decided to fight anyway. The Spanish governor in New Orleans had no men to spare, having sent them to take Florida from the British, so Leyba had to rely on the few soldiers and civilians he could muster from the surrounding countryside.

The commandant desperately called for recruits from the town and surrounding area but could come up with only 29 soldiers and 281 armed civilians. He also had several cannons. To protect St. Louis he built a tower he called Fort San Carlos and put the cannons on it so that they could cover the main northern approach to town. The tower is long gone, but it stood at the present-day intersection of Walnut and Fourth. For further protection he also had his men dig a trench around the town.

They finished just in time. On the morning of May 26, 1780, sixty-seven-year-old Pierre Raimond Quenel was fishing at the mouth of Cahokia Creek when he heard a noise on the opposite bank. Peering across the stream, he recognized Jean Marie Ducharme standing on the other side. Ducharme lived on the British side of the river and had been charged with hunting illegally in Spanish territory a few years before.

"Come over," Ducharme called, "I have something in particular to tell you."

Quenel noticed some Indians hiding in the bushes and immediately realized Ducharme was part of the invading army.

"No," he responded, "'though old and bald, yet I value my scalp too highly to trust myself with you."

Quenel hurried to his boat and paddled to St. Louis to warn Leyba. The commandant immediately collected his men and sent the women and children to hide in the governor's mansion. With an assistant pushing him around in a little cart, Leyba made a final check of the defenses and gave final orders to his tiny army.

Suddenly a large force of Indians burst from the forest north of the town, firing their guns and yelling war cries. The soldiers and civilians of St. Louis opened up with their muskets, and the cannons on the tower thundered away.

The Indians quickly retreated. They had assumed they'd have an easy victory against an almost defenseless foe, but instead found themselves attacking a fortified position. They soon regrouped and hid among the trees, keeping up continuous fire with their guns. As musket balls whizzed by, Leyba lay behind the defenses and shouted encouragement to his men. More practical help came from Madame Rigauche, a middle-aged woman who decided that she, too, should get to fight, grabbed a knife and pistol, and joined her husband in the trench. This display of bravery by a woman and a sick man emboldened the defenders, and they kept to their posts.

For two hours both sides exchanged fire until the Indians decided they didn't want to risk another frontal attack. Looking for easy prey, they looted the surrounding farms, killing or kidnapping everyone they met and destroying what they couldn't steal before disappearing into the forest and returning north.

St. Louis was saved, but twenty-one men, about half of them soldiers, lay dead. Seven of the dead were slaves who had been ordered to work in the unprotected fields, even though everyone knew an attack was imminent. Many other civilians suffered wounds or were taken prisoner for ransom. Only four Indians are known to have been killed.

Sadly, Leyba's illness grew worse, until on June 28 the victor of the Battle of Fort San Carlos, the westernmost battle of the American War of Independence, passed away. His successor came with more soldiers, improved the town's defenses, made peace with some tribes and raided others, and destroyed the British fort at St. Joseph, Michigan.

Now St. Louis was truly secure, and the area remained peaceful for the rest of the war. The United States of America soon became an independent, recognized nation, thanks in small part to the brave defenders of a town that wasn't even American yet.

LEWIS AND CLARK BRAVE
THE MISSOURI RIVER

1804

The three little wooden boats swayed and bucked through the rapid Missouri River current. Their crews desperately tried to steer away from rocks and sunken logs, which emerged like fangs from the frothing water. Although the two smaller craft, called pirogues, appeared frail on the dangerous Missouri, these flat-bottomed canoes were specially built for rough rivers. With a little determination and a lot of strength and courage, the men rowing the boats made it through the rapids.

The larger boat, however, a fifty-five-foot-long, eight-foot-wide keelboat that carried most of the men and supplies, struggled in the tenacious river, and the men discovered that this style of boat wasn't well suited to the wild waters of the Missouri. Too bad they had nearly two thousand miles more to travel.

But the commanders of this fleet, Captains Meriwether Lewis and William Clark, had been called to duty by the president of the United States, and they were determined. Thomas Jefferson had given them a mission to journey from St. Louis in the Louisiana Territory all the way to the Pacific Ocean in order to explore the newly purchased lands. The Louisiana Purchase, bought from the French, doubled the size of the United States overnight, but few Americans had explored it, and so Lewis, Clark, and a crew of forty-three soldiers, boatmen, and Clark's slave York set out to find a route to the West Coast and study the Indians, terrain, and natural resources along the way.

That is, if they could make it out of Missouri. It was early May, their first week of the journey, and they already faced danger. It was difficult to control the keelboat, which was caught on floating logs that made it impossible to handle. A weaker boat might have cracked like an eggshell, but the stout hull survived. After a few tense moments, the keelboat broke free, and all three boats made it through to calmer waters. The captains and crew of the Corps of Discovery wondered what other dangers they would face in the long journey ahead.

A few days later at St. Charles, a small settlement twenty-one miles upstream from St. Louis, the men made their first important discovery. They learned of two frontiersmen who wanted to go along with them. Both had mixed French and Omaha Indian heritage and a great deal of knowledge about the native peoples and the river. One of them was Pierre Cruzatte, who despite having the use of only one eye, and a nearsighted one to boot, proved to be an expert navigator.

On a treacherous river like the Missouri, such expertise could be lifesaving—more dangerous than the logs and currents were the so-called quick sandbars, little islands formed by currents that soon broke up and re-formed elsewhere, thus making them impossible to predict or map. Getting caught on those logs was only a taste of things to come.

The first serious test came on May 24, when they approached a wide section of the river cut into a maze of sandbars and shallow areas, with fast currents rushing between. Lewis and Clark feared getting caught in the shallows, but the only deep part was a narrow channel between the river's edge and an island, where a rough current broke off large chunks of the banks and hurled them into the water. Deciding it looked too dangerous, they crossed to the other side of the river, only to get the keelboat stuck on a sandbar. The current spun the boat around, nearly throwing the crew off their feet, and then it listed dangerously, threatening to capsize. Everyone ran to the far end, where their weight was enough to right the boat. But this also set the boat free, so that it spun around again and caught on another sandbar.

Desperate, some of the crew fastened one end of a rope to the stern, grabbed the other end, and dove into the water. Straining against strong, quick currents, they managed to swim to the riverbank and hauled the boat free before walking along shore and towing the boat into deeper waters. From there they decided to chance the narrow passage and finally made it through, exhausted by their adventure.

On June 9 the river was swollen and filled with logs after a prolonged downpour. The keelboat, durable but a bit hard to manage, got caught again, swinging around so that its long side faced the current. Logs shot downstream like arrows, ready to puncture the hull.

This time the crew was ready. Clark recorded in his journal for that day: "Some of our men being prepared for all Situations leaped into the water Swam ashore with a roap, and fixed themselves in Such Situations, that the boat was off in a fiew minits."

Bad spelling aside, Clark was clearly pleased with how his crew had already become experienced boatmen. When they passed the mouth of the Grand River and entered the 110-mile stretch between it and the mouth of the Kansas River, which everyone agreed was the toughest part of the Missouri, they were able to handle the boats with no accidents and make it to the Kansas River on June 26, having crossed the length of what would become the state of Missouri, 366 river miles, in forty-four days.

Lewis and Clark took notes on all they saw along the way, measuring the currents and mentioning the plentiful game in the area. Clark also proved how muddy the "Big Muddy" (as locals still call the river) could be. He filled a pint glass with river water and let it settle, drawing out half a wineglass of silt. This unusual unit of measurement wasn't terribly scientific, but it did show just how much dirt they drank with their water.

The crew suffered from fatigue, boils, ulcers, mosquitoes, and ticks, but they learned to act as a unit and handle the river like experts. This experience and teamwork, earned while still in Missouri, got them all the way to the Pacific and back, a distance of more than eight thousand miles. By the time they returned to St. Louis on September 23, 1806, they had grown into hardened explorers and carried journals filled with information about what lay in the land Jefferson had acquired for the nation.

Jefferson appointed Lewis governor of the Louisiana Territory, as the area was then called, and made Clark brigadier general of the territorial militia and Indian agent. Lewis had no taste for politics, and this, combined with political and financial troubles, pushed him into a deep depression. He committed suicide in 1809. Clark continued to work in the territory and served as the last territorial governor before Missouri became a state in 1820. Afterward he served as Indian agent and lived in St. Louis until his death in 1838, a popular and much-loved figure.

DANIEL BOONE'S
MISSOURI MISADVENTURE

1805

The three frontiersmen gazed out at the frozen Missouri River, weighing their chances of making it across. The late autumn weather had turned harsh, and they were anxious to get back to their warm cabin by Christmas. They had been gone a long time, hunting along the Gasconade River, and when they had reached this spot on the Missouri the day before, they found large floes of ice in the river, making it too dangerous to cross by canoe. During the night the temperature had dipped to below freezing, and they had woken up to see the river had frozen over.

With the morning sun providing no warmth in the bitter cold, all three examined the ice with expert eyes, for they were among the most experienced outdoorsmen on the American frontier. Leading them was a man already into his seventies and a living legend—Daniel Boone. Accompanying him were two of his sons, Daniel Morgan Boone and Nathan Boone.

Their conversation is lost to us, but it is likely that Nathan Boone recommended crossing the river. The previous Christmas he almost didn't get back for the holiday at all—he and a friend had been out hunting and had bagged fifty-six beavers and twelve otters when suddenly a band of Osage surrounded their camp. The Indian warriors took their horses and furs as retribution for hunting on their land. The next day another band of Indians, members of the Sauk tribe, robbed them of their blankets and coats. Exposed to the harsh elements and two hundred miles from home, they barely made it back alive.

Nathan must have shuddered at the thought of being caught out in the wilderness again, and he knew that getting back would please their wives, too. The women were accustomed to the hard life of the frontier but had never gotten used to their husbands leaving for long periods of time to have fun in the woods. Besides, Daniel Boone wasn't a young man anymore, and despite his rugged lifestyle his health was declining.

The Boones decided to chance it. They cut saplings into long poles and probed at the ice as they set out across the river. The younger men went first, followed by their father, with each adventurer carrying all of his supplies on his back. The furs, traps, food, ammunition, guns, and cooking and camping gear could add up to fifty pounds or more, so the possibility of plunging through the ice was very real.

With a sigh of relief, Daniel Morgan and Nathan made it to the north bank of the river, but just as they did, they heard an ominous crackling behind them, followed by a loud snap and a heart-stopping splash. They spun around and found their worst fears confirmed— their father had fallen through the ice!

Daniel Boone plunged up to his shoulders into frigid water and was soaked in an instant, the near-freezing river gripping him like the cold hand of death. Luckily he had fallen in not far from the north bank, and he could feel the muddy bottom of the river with his feet.

His head and arms were still above water and remained dry, but he knew that within minutes his body would numb and he'd slip under the surface, the current pulling him away under the ice, never to be seen again.

He struggled to lift himself up, but each time he tried, his weight cracked the ice around him and he splashed back in the water. Throwing a desperate glance at the shore, he saw his namesake, Daniel Morgan, coming over the ice to get him. He waved his son away, telling him to get back on shore. It wouldn't do for both of them to drown. Daniel Morgan could only stand there, watching his father's repeated attempts to get back on the ice, each one weaker than the last as the cold began to numb the old man.

Nathan took a more practical course of action. If his father made it out alive, he'd die soon enough without some warmth, so Nathan set about building a campfire.

Daniel Boone's knack for survival gave him the strength for one final attempt, and he made his way onto the ice again, spreading out his arms and legs so his body weight was dispersed. Fissures appeared all around him, and the squealing and crackling of the ice made his heart race, but the surface held. Hardly daring to breathe, he edged a little farther toward the shore. Every movement brought forth a protest from the ice, and at any moment he expected to plunge back into the river. Yet he kept edging toward his sons, his numb hands and shivering body giving every last ounce of their strength to make it to shore.

At last he reached it, and his two sons lifted him up. Nathan had built up a roaring bonfire, and he and his brother put their father right next to it. They stripped off his soaked clothing and wrapped him in spare blankets as his aged body was wracked with shivering.

After a time the shivering subsided. Daniel Boone lay swaddled in blankets next to the flames, slowly warming up. He was alive, but weak, and needed to get to proper shelter. Nathan and Daniel Morgan lifted him up again and carried him the few remaining miles back to their home.

Miraculously, Daniel Boone completely recovered from his unexpected swim in the Missouri River, and the old trailblazer lived another fifteen years. He must have had a good laugh about the incident over Christmas dinner with the family. It was another hazard of the wilderness that he had faced and overcome, and another tale to add to the rich storehouse of anecdotes about one of the most daring frontiersmen who ever lived.

FOUNDING FORT OSAGE

1808

When William Clark became Indian agent upon returning from the Corps of Discovery expedition, he inherited the task of dealing with the tribes in the new lands of the Louisiana Purchase. The various groups objected to American incursions on their traditional hunting and farming grounds, and occasionally raided outlying settlements. The tribes also sold furs to British merchants who snuck into the area to trade illegally.

The British took their furs north to Canada, while American merchants in St. Louis packed furs onto boats to sail down the Mississippi to New Orleans. Many spoiled on the way south, while those sent on the colder northern route stayed better preserved; thus the British merchants could afford to pay more. The Indians, not caring for American laws they had never asked for, did the practical thing and favored the highest bidder.

The most troublesome tribe was the Osage, a proud, warlike people and the most powerful tribe in the area. Osage warriors typically stood six feet or taller, at a time when the average European adult stood little over five feet. Raiding other tribes was a part of Osage culture, and young warriors eagerly set out to prove their bravery at the expense of their neighbors. The Osage dominated the fur trade and often dealt with British merchants from Canada. The Osage leader, White Hair, made peace with the new US government, but a chief was not an absolute ruler in the Osage culture, and many young warriors chose to ignore White Hair's commands.

This illicit trade hurt the fur merchants in St. Louis, many of whom were Clark's close friends and associates. Even worse, as more and more settlers intruded on Osage lands, the Indians' raids became more frequent and deadly. Clark needed to secure peace on the frontier.

The Osage were the only tribe not under Clark's jurisdiction. The Indian agent for the Osage was Pierre Chouteau, who had gained many years of experience with them when the area belonged to the French and Spanish. Chouteau wanted peace, too, but he had his own agenda.

In 1808 things took a turn for the worse when the Osage deposed White Hair. Now they felt free to raid at will, and soon bands of warriors attacked isolated farms, robbing and even killing a few settlers. To the government in St. Louis, this was savagery. To the Osage, however, this was self-defense.

Governor Lewis suspended trade with the tribe and announced they were no longer under US protection. The other tribes, who hated the Osage for their frequent attacks on them, started raiding Osage villages in retaliation. Surrounded by enemies, cut off from trade with the Americans, and having little chance to trade with the British in such a chaotic situation, the Osage had no choice but to negotiate.

This is exactly what Clark had hoped for. He offered the Osage a deal—the raids and illegal trading would stop, and in return they would get a trading post (called a "factory" in those days) in their territory. Clark had already examined a likely spot when he had passed up the Missouri River in 1804. About three hundred miles upriver from where it met the Mississippi, a high bluff offered a commanding view of the river and surrounding area. It lay in the heart of Osage lands, unlike the older factory at Fort Belle Fontaine, which stood just four miles from the meeting of the two rivers and well within the area of American settlement.

In August 1808 the first group of workers set out to establish the fort and factory. Clark and a company of dragoons followed close behind, riding overland with Nathan Boone, son of Daniel Boone, as a guide. Once they got to the fort, Boone went to inform the Osage that construction had started. A tribal delegation soon arrived to make peace with the Americans. In return for access to the fort and factory, the Osage gave up their land between the Missouri and Arkansas Rivers. They were already losing it to illegal settlers, so giving it to the government would ease tensions between the Indians and the newcomers.

But the Osage tradition of having leaders with only limited power soon caused trouble. Another tribal delegation showed up in St. Louis saying they disagreed with the treaty and wanted to renegotiate.

Clark suspected that Chouteau had a hand in this. Chouteau wanted the government to approve his claim to a large area of land he said had been given to him when Spain ruled the area. Others had similar claims. Most didn't have the proper paperwork, and some claims conflicted with others, so the Spanish land claim issue had become a major controversy, with the claims tied up in the courts. Clark felt Chouteau was getting his Osage friends to cause trouble in order to reword the treaty so that it recognized his claim. Clark's suspicions became certainty when Chouteau himself suggested the change.

Clark had to do some fast talking to convince Chouteau that his personal real estate problems were not going to be covered in an Indian treaty and managed to induce him to take a revised treaty to the Osage. The new document promised that the factory would include a blacksmith shop and a mill to provide the Osage with metal tools and flour. They would also get $1,500 every year. The surrender of land and the promise of government protection remained in the treaty.

These provisions satisfied everyone, except for Chouteau, and on November 10, 1808, the two parties signed the agreement at the new fort, named Fort Osage. It is said the warlike Osage danced all night in celebration of their peace with the Americans and the profitable trade they would now enjoy. For a time Fort Osage was the western-most military post of the United States, at the edge of official control, and its combination of economic benefit and military power kept the peace. Its presence reassured settlers heading farther west, but its own success led to its closure. By 1827 it no longer stood at the frontier. Two years before, the government had removed the Osage to a reservation in Kansas, and settlers rushed into their old lands. Although the fort lasted only nineteen years, it had a major impact on Missouri's development.

THE NEW MADRID EARTHQUAKE

1811

In the early-morning hours of December 16, 1811, the citizens of the little town of New Madrid on the Mississippi River were thrown from their beds. Their houses shook violently, cracks appeared in their brick chimneys, and everything on the shelves cascaded to the floor. Outside in the barns all the animals began to bleat and howl. The residents of New Madrid had woken up to an earthquake.

People fled into the cold night, grabbing whatever clothes they could in the rush to escape their trembling houses. Once they were outside, they huddled together for warmth and security, hoping and praying they would live to see sunrise. Every few minutes there was another tremor, and the terrified pioneers wondered if it would ever stop.

As dawn broke, the ground shook with another great tremor, and the settlers witnessed the ground undulating like waves lapping the shore. Rifts opened up in the earth, belching forth debris and the nauseating smell of sulfur. An even stronger tremor hit at 11:00 a.m.

Despite the fact that few people lived in the area at the time, there were several casualties. One woman was crushed by her falling cabin.

A man fell into a hole in the earth and was never seen again. Two more settlers died from shock and exposure. A half dozen Indians drowned when the riverbank sloughed off into the raging Mississippi.

Boatmen on the Mississippi fared even worse. While the land trembled, the river churned like a pot of water shaken back and forth. Boats overturned or smashed against rocks, and untold numbers of boatmen disappeared into the water.

As the day advanced, people saw the full extent of the damage. Their houses lay in ruins, many of their animals were dead or had run off, and most of the trees in the surrounding wilderness had fallen down. Great chasms in the earth impeded the refugees' passage. They found themselves stranded in a surreal wilderness, on a frontier with no roads and miles away from any help.

Nor was that the end of their suffering. As they set up makeshift shelters to get out of the cold or trudged their weary way to St. Louis or other distant towns, they had to endure more quakes and tremors. On January 23 came a full-scale earthquake just as bad as the first, followed by another bad one on February 4, and the worst of them all on February 7. The final quake threw people off their feet while the waters of the Mississippi receded, leaving terrified sailors stuck in the muddy river bottom, desperately struggling to reach shore before the river came back. The earthquake was so strong that it damaged houses in Cincinnati, four hundred miles away, and could even be felt in the nation's capital, a distance of almost eight hundred miles. In St. Louis several stone houses cracked in two.

According to popular folklore the river flowed backward for three days. While this is a bit of an exaggeration, there is an element of truth to the story. When fissures or breaks appeared in the riverbed, they created waterfalls. Sometimes the riverbed upstream ended up being lower than the portion downstream, so sections of the river would flow backward for a short time before the pressure and flow of the water reasserted itself. Just as dangerous to boatmen were the numerous waterspouts, whirlpools, and collapsing riverbanks created by the shaking river. Dozens of boats are known to have sunk, and many more probably slipped unreported into the deep.

The river washed away the following towns: Little Prairie, which became known as the "Lost Village"; an Indian town a few miles south of New Madrid; and New Madrid itself. New Madrid stood on a bend in the river, and the north bank of this bend eroded nearly a mile, taking the old town with it. All but two families moved away from the area, and it would be some time before the new New Madrid would become a town again . . . a mile north of its original location.

A few years later, in 1815, the federal government offered free land to those uprooted by the quake, but most victims had already left the region, and dishonest people claiming to be from the affected area took most of the free land. This swindling of the government became a great controversy, and for many years the term "New Madrid claim" was synonymous with any sort of dishonest dealing.

The rural nature of the region kept the death toll from being higher, but the area is much more populated nowadays. New Madrid currently has a population of more than three thousand. Seismologists still worry about what they call the New Madrid Seismic Zone. In 1990 local residents were treated to two tremors, measuring 4.6 and 3.6 on the Richter scale, a scale ranging from 1 to 10 that scientists use to measure the strength of an earthquake. No one was seriously hurt in those quakes. The New Madrid earthquake of 1811, on the other hand, was probably more than 8 on the Richter scale. Seismologists hope there will never again be one that bad.

A STATE IN THE MAKING

1818–1821

Missourians were outraged. Ever since the Louisiana Purchase made them part of the United States, they had been a territory and not a state. Now, after years of hard work, they enjoyed a thriving economy and an expanding population, and they felt it was time to become a state, one among equals with the twenty-two other states in the Union. But a congressman from New York was trying to stop that from happening.

House Speaker Henry Clay of Kentucky submitted a request for Missouri statehood, saying that its population numbered just less than 100,000. While this was a bit of an exaggeration (the population actually stood at about 66,500), Missouri had certainly become a viable enough entity to qualify as a state. Missouri's territorial delegate John Scott got the House to form a Committee of the Whole to authorize the territory to create its own state government.

Then came trouble. Missouri's population included about ten thousand slaves, and Northern politicians, led by James Tallmadge Jr. of New York, didn't want new slave states because it would tip the balance of power in favor of the South. The number of representatives a state could send to the House depended on its population, and while slaves had no political rights, the Constitution said they counted as three-fifths of a person when calculating a state's population. Many Northerners also had moral objections to slavery, and the rising importance of black voters in some free states, especially New York, couldn't be ignored.

Tallmadge got the committee to add an amendment banning the importation of slaves to Missouri and making all children born of slaves already in Missouri free once they turned twenty-five. The vote in the House over the revised bill broke down along geographical lines, with almost all Southern representatives voting against it because of the Tallmadge Amendment and most Northerners voting in favor. The ratio of Northerners and Southerners in the Senate was equal because each state had two senators and there were eleven Southern states and eleven Northern ones, but the proslavery faction managed to defeat the Tallmadge Amendment with the help of some sympathetic Northerners. Missouri's statehood bill, without the amendment, went back to the House, where it was rejected. When the Fifteenth Congress adjourned, Missouri's status remained unresolved. But the battle wasn't even close to completion.

John Scott pointed out that the treaty of cession transferring the region from France to the United States stipulated that the territory's inhabitants should be admitted as soon as possible as full citizens of the United States and that their property, which included slaves, had to be protected.

Readers deluged the territory's newspapers with their opinions. Most favored unrestricted admission. Only a single newspaper, the *St. Louis Missouri Gazette & Public Advertiser,* edited by Joseph Charless, was bold enough to publish opposing viewpoints. One writer—who timidly, but perhaps wisely, signed his letter only as "A Farmer of St. Charles County"—noted that the wording of the treaty of cession said that all "inhabitants" should become US citizens, and surely slaves counted as inhabitants. The author of the letter laughed at the slaveholders who said the rule freeing the children of slaves reduced their value by comparing these slaveholders to a tavern keeper who "when a traveler obtained from him a dinner of eggs, charged him with the price of all hens and chickens which *might have been* produced from those eggs to the end of time."

When the battle went before Congress again, the northern part of Massachusetts asked to be admitted as the state of Maine. This led to the possibility for compromise. Maine wanted to be a free state; so if Missouri was admitted as a slave state, the balance of power in Congress would be maintained. The House passed a bill approving Maine's application and sent it to the Senate, where an amendment was added approving Missouri's unrestricted admission. Senator J. B. Thomas of Illinois added another amendment ruling that all Louisiana Purchase lands north of 36°30', the southern boundary of Missouri, would be free and that those below it could legally have slaves. The one exception was Missouri, which could have slaves. The amended bill passed the Senate easily and went back to the House.

The amendment was an attempt to reconcile both sides. The division of Louisiana Purchase lands allowed the slave economy to expand westward while leaving most of the West as free territory. Moderates on both sides eagerly supported what became known as the Missouri Compromise. They worried about the increasingly radical talk of some congressmen, which included even a few mentions of secession, and this compromise seemed to offer the best way out.

But opponents in the House had their way and rejected the bill, and they added their own amendment banning slavery in

Missouri completely. At this point moderates in both the Senate and the House organized. Henry Clay formed a committee reintroducing the bill with the Missouri Compromise attached. With a lot of convincing of hard-liners on both sides, he got it passed and sent it on to President James Monroe, who signed it into law on March 6, 1820.

Back in Missouri the people rejoiced. Bands played, people drank numerous toasts to Clay and Scott, and bonfires blazed through the night, surrounded by revelers thrilled that they would soon become full citizens of the United States.

They celebrated too early. When Missouri's counties elected delegates to attend a state constitutional convention, they elected only proslavery men, reflecting the majority opinion. The constitutional convention put no restriction on slavery and created no timetable for its abolition, which the liberal *Gazette* editor Joseph Charless had recommended. Indeed, the convention actually made it illegal to free slaves without paying the master and getting his consent and forbade free blacks from moving into Missouri.

This last item was just what the hard-line restrictionists in Congress were looking for. Despite the fact that Delaware had a similar law, they claimed it was unconstitutional for one state to limit the free movement of a citizen of another state and rejected Missouri's admission.

Once again Henry Clay had to cool heads and bring about a reconciliation. He got Congress to agree to approve Missouri's statehood on the condition the state pass a "Solemn Public Act" proclaiming that the restriction on the entry of black people would never be enforced. On June 26, 1821, Missouri's General Assembly passed the act, and on August 10 President Monroe formally made Missouri a state. This kicked off a new round of celebrations in Missouri and a profound sense of relief everywhere else.

Missourians gleefully held their first elections and rewarded territorial delegate John Scott by electing him Missouri's first representative in the House.

But not everyone celebrated. An aging Thomas Jefferson had watched the acrimonious debate over slavery with a growing sense of unease. Although a slaveholder himself, he had never been comfortable with the institution and predicted the division and mistrust between slave states and free states would lead to the destruction of the Union. Forty years later his prediction came true.

A GERMAN IN MISSOURI

1829

The leaky old wooden ship tossed and swayed through the rough Atlantic waters, mercilessly rocking its seasick passengers. Down in the hold, a few hundred Germans moaned and coughed, wondering when their ordeal would be over. Families huddled together, and parents hugged their children as they asked for the thousandth time when they would get to Missouri, the Promised Land somewhere on the other side of the stormy sea.

Some would never make it. Disease was rife in the crowded ship, and already a few berths lay empty after their occupants had succumbed to pneumonia or flu. Their beds now served as storage spaces, providing the survivors with a bit of extra room to move around.

Despite their suffering, the passengers remained optimistic. Many clutched copies of the latest bestseller, *Report on a Journey to the Western States of North America* by Gottfried Duden.

Duden was a Prussian lawyer who had spent three years living in what is now Warren County, where he bought a farm and marveled at Missouri's green hills and lush forests. His writings exult in the fine land he found:

> *I cannot describe the impression that the days of wan-*
> *dering in this river valley have made upon me. One can*
> *travel hundreds of miles between gigantic tree trunks*
> *without a single ray of sunlight falling upon one's head.*
> *The soil is so black here from the plant mold that has*
> *been accumulating since primeval days that one seems*
> *to be walking on a coal bed. I have seen grape vines*
> *whose trunks, over a foot thick, rise up about a hundred*
> *feet, free as cables, and then spread out in the crowns of*
> *elms with their heavily foliaged vines.*

Many such passages fill his book, which, when published in 1829, became an instant success, enticing readers with its colorful language and detailed instructions on how to immigrate.

To the Germans, Duden's descriptions sounded like paradise. Germany wasn't a unified country at the time but was instead a patchwork of smaller states that often fought one another. The nobility owned most of the land, and farmers had to work their vast estates in exchange for a small fraction of the harvest. Commoners had few opportunities for advancement, and so Missouri sounded ideal.

After a grueling three-month voyage, the ship landed at New Orleans. The exhausted immigrants were nearly knocked out by the hot, humid climate and hurried to buy tickets for riverboats headed up the Mississippi. After another week of travel, they finally reached St. Louis, finding a bustling town full of opportunity. Some decided to stay, joining the growing German population and getting jobs in the many German-owned businesses. Some of those who had saved a little extra money opened up businesses themselves, but most of the new Americans headed west to buy farms in the rich lands Duden had written about.

They soon had their illusions shattered. Duden had lived a sheltered life. Because he didn't know anything about farming, he had hired Americans to work his fields while he traveled around the region taking notes. He also enjoyed unusually fine weather during his stay, suffering none of the sudden biting snowstorms and sweltering muggy summers that pioneers (and modern Missourians) had to endure.

Clearing the land was tough work, and the boiling summers and frigid winters were nowhere to be found in Duden's account. Some moved back to join their friends in St. Louis, but many stuck it out and soon achieved their dream of owning their own farm, something almost impossible to do back home.

The new arrivals preferred to keep their own culture, and before long the land alongside the Missouri River was dotted with villages that looked as though they had been shipped over from Germany, complete with German beer halls, German schools, and German churches. The farmers found that while some of the land wasn't as good as they had hoped, grapes can flourish where many other crops cannot, and soon rich vineyards spread out along the river.

While Duden never really understood life here, his confidence that it would be a good home for his compatriots turned out to be correct. In the decades following the publication of his book, tens of thousands of his fellow Germans settled in the state, contributing to its development and prosperity.

A SLAVE SUES FOR HIS FREEDOM

1846–1856

In April 1846, a slave named Dred Scott walked into a St. Louis courthouse and filed suit against his owner, Irene Emerson, claiming he wasn't a slave at all. He also stated that his wife, Harriet, and two daughters, Eliza and Lizzie, were also free. The clerk at the court office must have been astounded. Slaves rarely sued their masters, and the evidence in support of Scott's case was rarer still—it was his life story.

Scott was born a slave in Virginia around 1800. His first master, Peter Blow, moved to St. Louis in 1830 and soon sold Scott to Dr. John Emerson, a US Army surgeon, who took him to Fort Armstrong in Illinois. Illinois was a free state, but Scott was apparently unaware that merely by living there he could claim his freedom.

Dr. Emerson later transferred to Fort Snelling, in what is now Minnesota. This area, then part of the Wisconsin Territory, was also free. Once again Scott appeared unaware of the law, and no one tried to relieve Emerson of his "property."

During his stay in the Wisconsin Territory, Scott married another slave, Harriet Robinson. Her master was a justice of the peace and married the two in a civil ceremony. Marriage was not allowed in slave states, which did not recognize slave marriages as legally binding. Emerson transferred back to St. Louis but hired out his slaves for a time in Fort Snelling, an illegal act in a free territory. The doctor moved again, this time to Louisiana, where he married Eliza Irene Sanford and sent for his slaves.

Soon the group headed back to Fort Snelling, and during the trip Harriet gave birth to the Scotts' first daughter, Eliza. The delivery occurred on the Mississippi River between Illinois and the Wisconsin Territory, both free areas. The group later returned to St. Louis, where Dr. Emerson died.

After his death Dr. Emerson's widow rented out her slaves. In 1846 Scott tried to buy freedom for himself and his family, which soon included a second daughter, Lizzie. Irene Emerson wasn't interested in giving them up, however, and Scott decided to sue.

His suit was funded by the sons of his former master, Peter Blow, who wanted to free the man they used to play with as children. The case appeared strong. Dred Scott had spent considerable time in free areas, his master had broken the law by renting him out in one such area, Scott's marriage to Harriet had been confirmed by a civil ceremony reserved for free people, Harriet had also spent considerable time in free areas, and their first daughter was born in a free area. If they were free, then their second daughter was also free by virtue of being born to free parents. There was even legal precedent—courts in several slave states had liberated slaves who had resided in free areas.

At first Scott was stymied by a technicality. The St. Louis circuit court threw out his case because he had no witnesses to prove Irene Emerson owned him. A new trial eventually began in 1850, and this time the judge ruled in Scott's favor, but Emerson appealed to the state Supreme Court.

At this point Scott ran into trouble. Chief Justice William Scott ruled:

> *[N]ot only individuals but States have been possessed with a dark and fell [malevolent] spirit in relation to slavery, whose gratification is sought in the pursuit of measures, whose inevitable consequence must be the overthrow and destruction of our Government. Under such circumstances, it does not behoove the State of Missouri to show the least countenance to any measure which might gratify this spirit. (*Scott vs. Emerson, *15 Mo. 576 [1852], 586)*

This decision denied the family's freedom in order to avoid trouble between slave and free states. While it was a political rather than a legal decision, Chief Justice William Scott's prediction proved correct. A civil war was in the offing, and this case would help lead the country into it.

Scott now went to federal court. His tenacity was beginning to draw attention from the press, and he became a *cause célèbre* among abolitionists. Irene Emerson had since moved away and remarried, so now Dred Scott had to fight Irene's brother, John Sanford, who claimed authority over the Scotts.

Scott sued Sanford in the US Circuit Court for wrongful imprisonment, stating that he was forced into slavery. He also sued for $9,000 because Sanford had hit him. Sanford claimed that a black man was not a citizen of Missouri and therefore couldn't sue in federal court, but the court rejected this argument.

The case was heard in May 1854, and the court followed the reasoning of the lower court and ruled that the Scotts were slaves. But Dred Scott had too much at stake to give up. He now headed to the US Supreme Court, which heard the case in February 1856.

At that time the nine Supreme Court justices included three slave owners and two more who came from slave-owning families. The chief justice, Roger Taney, came from a big tobacco-growing family that owned many slaves.

The opinion Taney formulated in the case, which all but two justices agreed with, was a radical one. He ruled that blacks weren't citizens of the United States, despite being state citizens, but decided that his court would hear the case anyway. He even said that blacks were "so far inferior . . . that they had no rights which the white man was bound to respect" (*Dred Scott*, 19 How. 407).

Then Taney stated that the federal government couldn't rule on slavery in the territories, despite the Constitution's provision that "Congress shall have Power to dispose of and make all needful Rules and Regulations respecting the Territory or other Property belonging to the United States." Taney reasoned that this applied only to territories owned when the Constitution was approved in 1787. He furthermore stated that banning slavery, or freeing slaves who went to a free territory, deprived people of their property in violation of the Fifth Amendment. Even the people of a territory couldn't vote to abolish slavery, since it went against the constitutional right to own slaves. Dred Scott would remain a slave.

It was clear to everyone this decision was a political one. Just two days before, President-elect James Buchanan, a staunch supporter of slavery, said the future of slavery needed to be decided by the courts and that he would abide by the result. Many Northerners, especially Republicans, were outraged. A junior politician named Abraham Lincoln claimed that Taney and the Court were conspiring with Buchanan and other Democrats to spread slavery throughout the United States. Indeed, records show Buchanan was kept informed of the case's developments, so he knew which way the ruling would go when he made his speech. Many Northerners feared there would be another case ruling that if slaves were not free even in free states, then slavery was legal everywhere.

In the end, Northern fear surrounding the ramifications of the Dred Scott case helped Lincoln win the 1860 presidential election, leading to the secession of the Southern states and the Civil War.

And Dred Scott? After the ruling the Blow family purchased the Scotts and freed them on May 26, 1857. Sadly, Dred Scott died less than nine months later. He enjoyed his freedom for only a short time, but his tireless fight was a major cause of the war that freed his people.

THE *SALUDA* DISASTER

1852

Captain Francis Belt looked at his steamboat docked at the St. Louis levee and shook his head in frustration. It was March 26, and the *Saluda* had been sitting idle too long. A late thaw on the Missouri River meant he couldn't make his usual route. He and the ship's bartender, Peter Conrad, were joint owners of the boat, and the delay cut into their personal finances. It must have been a huge relief when two strangers approached the beleaguered captain asking for passage.

Eli Kelsey and David Ross worked as agents of the Church of Jesus Christ of Latter-day Saints, popularly known as Mormons, to assist its members in crossing the country to Utah. Several hundred Mormons had just arrived in St. Louis that day, and Kelsey and Ross were hoping the down-on-his-finances Captain Belt would be interested in carrying the church members upriver.

Belt leapt at the chance. He agreed to take almost a hundred of the Mormons and told them the ship would depart on March 30, ice or no ice.

The *Saluda* had been running the rivers for six years, but with a less than stellar record. Six years in service was a long time for a steamboat, and it had already sunk and been raised once. The engines and the two boilers, however, had sunk twice. They had been salvaged from the wreck of an earlier steamboat. Kelsey and Ross could have picked a better boat with their eyes closed.

Their destination was Kanesville, now known as Council Bluffs, 783 miles up the Missouri in Iowa. Kanesville was the main launching point for Mormons headed to Utah, and Captain Belt planned to stop at several towns along the way to pick up and drop off passengers and cargo.

By the middle of the nineteenth century, hundreds of steamboats paddled their way up the Mississippi and Missouri Rivers every year, carrying passengers and cargo to dozens of riverside towns. Both rivers could be dangerous, with changing currents, sandbars, and hidden logs, but the worst danger sat right in the boat itself—the boiler that powered the steam engine. A weakness in the iron or a sudden buildup of pressure could result in an explosion, and since few boilers had pressure gauges, engineers had to rely on experience and guesswork to keep the boat safe. Using old boilers that had twice seen the bottom of the river was nothing short of suicidal.

Although many died in steamboat accidents, it was still the fastest and most convenient way to travel in the days before trains became common, and many passengers joined the Mormons on board, eager to start their journey upriver.

At first all went well. The boat made good time and arrived at Lexington, 372 miles upriver, on April 4. But when the crew tried to steer her around Lexington Bend, a swiftly flowing curve in the river, the *Saluda*'s boiler and engines couldn't put out enough power to push her through. Captain Belt finally gave up and docked at Lexington, deciding to try again the next day. On the second attempt the boat hit chunks of ice and damaged the paddle wheels, forcing a return to Lexington for repairs. Some of the wealthier passengers left in disgust. Captain Miller of the *Isabel,* just arrived from St. Louis, took one look at the *Saluda* and docked his own boat as far away as possible. To his experienced eyes the *Saluda* looked like a floating time bomb.

The Mormon passengers must have felt uncomfortable, too. Less than twenty years before, in the so-called Mormon War of 1838, many of their brethren had been killed in a mass removal of Mormons from Missouri. Missourians had mistrusted the large number of immigrants from the unfamiliar new faith and wanted to be rid of them. In a series of raids and skirmishes, people on both sides died, but the Mormons suffered the most, losing their homes, farms, and most of their possessions. Although Mormons were now supposedly safe in Missouri, the passengers wouldn't feel comfortable until they crossed the state line.

By April 9 the crew had finished the repairs, most of the ice was gone, and Captain Belt announced they would leave that morning.

Local folklore says that as the *Saluda* pulled away from the levee, Captain Belt shouted to Captain Miller, "I will round the point this morning or I will blow this boat to Hell!"

Desperate for more speed, Belt ordered his second engineer, Josiah Clancey, to add cold water to the hot but almost-empty boilers. This would make the water steam up in an instant, adding a surge of power to the engines. But the sudden increase in pressure was more than the tired old boilers could handle, and both burst in a terrible twin explosion.

Almost the entire upper half of the boat shattered into thousands of pieces and flew high into the air. Captain Belt was hurled over the levee and fell to the ground, dead. Clancey was thrown onto the shore but lived long enough to explain what happened. Peter Conrad was badly scalded by the steam but survived. Others were not so lucky. Some died instantly from the explosion, or died as they plummeted into the water or onto dry land. The flying debris even killed a man standing on the riverbank.

The citizens of Lexington rushed to help the survivors. Doctors treated those who had been blown ashore but still lived, and locals boarded rowboats and hurried across the water to the wreckage. Passengers and crew clung to floating bits of hull, while others remained trapped inside the lower part of the boat as it rapidly sank.

The citizens of Lexington managed to save them all. They even fished David Ross out of the river, where he had been flung by the explosion and managed to keep afloat until help came. One tale claims a baby was found hanging unhurt from a tree and another baby was found alive a mile downstream, where it had floated in its crib. While the truth of the last two stories is a bit dubious, everyone who survived must have thought they had been saved by a miracle. Some survivors had a more terrestrial savior to thank—Thaddeus Huff, a seventeen-year-old boy who swam back and forth from the wreck to the shore three times, carrying members of his family to safety.

The disintegrating pieces of the *Saluda* sank or floated away, and soon little remained of the boat except for what blew ashore. The town of Lexington raised money to bury the dead and care for the injured. Captain Miller offered free passage on the *Isabel* for anyone ready to continue their journey. Local families adopted some of the orphaned children.

Because the passenger list was partially destroyed and some of the bodies disappeared into the water, it is unclear how many died, but historians estimate between seventy-five and one hundred, making it the worst steamboat disaster on the Missouri. Many more suffered serious injuries. The *Saluda* tragedy had left an ominous mark on steamboat travel.

Later that same week two other steamboats exploded, one on the St. Louis levee and the other on the Ohio River; combined, the two explosions claimed eighty lives. Later that year the government passed strict new safety regulations for steamboats, including the installation of pressure gauges. Although the *Saluda* was not the last disaster on the Missouri River, steamboat travel became much safer.

If the Mormon survivors worried about how the Missourians would treat them, their minds were soon easily put to rest. All were given the best of care, no matter what their faith. William Dunbar, who lost his wife and children in the disaster, had his wounds treated in the home of a man who sheepishly admitted he had helped evict Mormons in 1838. The past was soon forgotten in the face of a common tragedy.

THE PONY EXPRESS SETS OUT

1860

On April 3, 1860, the citizens of St. Joseph waited impatiently to see a historic occasion. Gentlemen checked their pocket watches as women in bonnets peered down the empty street. Local farmers in dusty overalls joked with one another and traded skeptical looks as the wait stretched long and longer. Small children, feeling the energy of the crowd, played and ran in the excitement of the moment.

The Pony Express, the first rapid mail service to California, would set out that night. Everything was prepared. The company of Russell, Majors, and Waddell had set up nearly two hundred relay stations approximately every ten miles from Missouri to California, staffed with horses and riders so that the mail could be put on a fresh horse, which could then gallop to the next station without a stop. The citizens had raised flags on every rooftop, and red, white, and blue colors decorated the buildings near the stable. The mayor had prepared a speech. The first rider and horse stood ready. Everything was in place for a 5:00 p.m. departure except for one vital ingredient—the mail.

Some messages had already arrived by telegraph, and now the town waited for a special delivery of mail coming from the East Coast, including special editions of newspapers (one printed on tissue paper since the service's high rates were based on weight) and a letter from President Buchanan to Governor Downey of California. But the courier had missed his train in Detroit and got delayed. He had finally made it to Hannibal, but that was on the other side of the state.

J. T. K. Haywood, superintendent of the Hannibal–St. Joseph railroad, realized the eyes of the nation were fixed on Missouri and decided to help. He commissioned the steam engine *Missouri* to pull one carriage to take the messenger across the state. He ordered all other trains off the line and all the switches spiked closed so the train could have an uninterrupted race across Missouri. It would be the first US train to run for the sole purpose of carrying mail.

As the courier hustled on board, engineer Addison "Ad" Clark and his assistants stoked the fire in the engine to build up a strong head of steam. The engine chugged as great plumes of smoke belched from the smokestack. Clark blew the whistle, and the train pulled out of Hannibal station to the cheers of the crowd.

Clark and his men were off and running. Through Marion, Ralls, Monroe, and Shelby Counties, they kept up a pace of sixty miles an hour, a breakneck speed for the time. News of the race across the state had flashed along the telegraph wires, and crowds flocked to the tracks to cheer them on. As the train approached Macon, the land became hilly, with the track making hard turns along steep grades. Clark hardly even slowed down. The heavy locomotive swerved around the turns, barely keeping its wheels on the tracks.

As the train approached Macon, Clark slammed on the brakes and screeched to a halt in L. S. Coleman's wood yard to refuel. Coleman knew he was coming and had built up a platform to the level of the train's tender, where the wood fuel for the steam engine was kept. The moment Clark stopped, a row of men stepped forward and dumped armfuls of wood into the tender. This refueling didn't take long, and before he knew it, the engine was ready to go.

Just outside Macon was a steep grade down to the Chariton River. Clark took it at full speed, his train looking like an avalanche of iron as fire shot out of the smokestack and sparks flew everywhere. Clark shot over the railroad bridge and off to the west.

Over in St. Joseph the crowd grew antsy. The mayor and the company representative had made their speeches, and everyone milled around, wondering if the mail would make it. Then, at around 7:00 p.m., the long, shrill wail of a train whistle echoed from the east. Everyone cheered. Within moments the *Missouri* pulled into the station, having made the run in a record of four hours and fifty-one minutes. Clark and his crew, covered in soot, waved from the engine as the courier stepped onto the platform. The horse was retrieved from the stable, where it had been hiding after the crowd had clipped off most of its tail for souvenirs, and a young rider named Bill Richardson mounted, grabbed the mail, and galloped away by 7:15 p.m.

Richardson's older brother managed the stable and gave him the honor of being the first rider. The company, however, thought he was too young to make the run, so when he rode down to the Missouri River, Johnny Frye, a champion rider, took the horse and crossed to the other bank on a steamboat. As soon as the boat docked on the other side, Frye urged his mount to a gallop and disappeared into the night. Ten days later, the rider on the other end of the relay system delivered the mail to San Francisco, right on schedule. Another package of mail heading to St. Joseph had left San Francisco at the same time, and it, too, arrived on time. The Pony Express was off and running.

The Pony Express delivered mail from St. Joseph to San Francisco, a distance of 1,840 miles, in ten days, twice as fast as the old

Butterfield stagecoach route. People on the East Coast could send telegraph messages to St. Joseph, which would then be relayed by the express riders, tough young men who rode across sparsely settled territory, facing hostile Indians, barren deserts, and extremes of weather to get the mail through. One recruiting poster for the Pony Express read, "Wanted: Young skinny, wiry fellows not over eighteen. Must be expert riders, willing to risk death daily. Orphans preferred." Despite this rather discouraging help-wanted ad, hundreds of young men in search of adventure clamored to join the service. Only the best were chosen.

On October 24, 1861, however, the first transcontinental telegraph line reached California, and the Pony Express lost its reason to exist. It ceased operation two days later, after only nineteen months in business, but it became an enduring chapter in the story of the West.

THE FIRST CIVIL WAR SHOTS
IN MISSOURI

1861

The late spring sunshine warmed the faces of bankers, blacksmiths, women, and children as another fine day dawned in St. Louis. Workers headed out to their jobs and storekeepers opened their doors. Down at the docks, dozens of steamboats unloaded their cargoes. Everything seemed right in the prosperous city. But underneath this tranquility people were troubled. The election of Abraham Lincoln the previous November had caused the Southern states to secede and create the Confederate States of America. In April, rebel batteries bombarded Fort Sumter in Charleston Harbor and forced the Federal troops stationed there to surrender. North and South were now at war.

But in Missouri the question remained: Which side would the state take? On the one hand, much of the rural population had originally come from Southern states such as Tennessee, Virginia, and the Carolinas and sympathized with the Southern cause. On the other hand, St. Louis and other big towns had a large number of European immigrants and Northerners who disliked slavery and wanted

Missouri to follow the more industrial, less agricultural economy the North provided.

Even the Missouri legislature couldn't agree. Earlier in the year a state convention had voted to stay in the Union as long as the North didn't "coerce" the South, but Southern sympathizers pointed out that Lincoln had called for a huge army of volunteers to fight the new Confederacy. Wasn't that coercion of the worst kind? Missouri governor Claiborne Jackson publicly refused to send a single man to Lincoln's army.

Secessionists started Minute Men committees, named after the famous fighters of the American War of Independence, to fight for the Confederacy when the time came. Union men, especially the large German population in St. Louis, formed Home Guard units and drilled in the streets.

As people argued back and forth, the leaders of both sides got ready to fight. Governor Jackson and his vice-governor, Thomas Reynolds, secretly applied to Confederate President Jefferson Davis for military aid. Meanwhile, Nathaniel Lyon, the Union officer in charge of the defense of St. Louis, encouraged loyalists to form more militias.

Both sides eyed the city's arsenal, filled with barrels of gunpowder, thirty thousand guns, and other supplies. Whoever controlled that would be able to create an army.

Brigadier General Daniel Frost, commander of the state militia for the St. Louis area, rode into this explosive situation. He led about seven hundred men, supposedly there for their regularly scheduled practice maneuvers but really determined to take the arsenal and supply a rebel army to capture the state. Many of these men were members of the Minute Men companies. They made camp at Lindell Grove and boasted of what they would do to the "Damned Dutch," as they contemptuously called the German Unionists. They named their bivouac Camp Jackson in honor of the secessionist governor and put up street signs between the tents with the names of prominent rebels such as "Jefferson Davis" and "Beauregard," the rebel commander who had bombarded Fort Sumter.

Lyon immediately suspected the militia's intentions. Some tell the tale that he dressed up as a woman and rode through Camp Jackson to spy on it, but since he had a red beard at the time, this anecdote is a bit hard to believe. Others say he snuck into camp (in men's clothes) by crawling along a ditch. Whichever story is true, Lyon decided the militia must be stopped. His last doubts, if the fanatically Unionist officer had had any in the first place, were extinguished when he discovered a shipment of mortars and cannons on the docks of St. Louis, hidden in boxes labeled "marble." They had been sent to Frost by Jefferson Davis. Lyon quietly moved most of the arsenal's contents across the river to the pro-Union state of Illinois.

On May 10 Frost's militia was due to go home and had not made any move against the arsenal, but Lyon felt sure they would attack soon. Lyon was determined to make a show of force and nip the rebellion in the bud, so he marched to Lindell Grove with a battalion of regular soldiers and four regiments of German Home Guards (nearly eight thousand men), surrounded the camp, and demanded its surrender.

Frost had little choice. He was outnumbered and cut off, and even if he made a stand, Lyon could bring thousands more troops from the city to crush him. After a few minutes' thought, he gave up. Flush with easy victory, Lyon dismounted to receive the surrender and promptly got kicked in the stomach by a horse.

Lyon picked himself up and pretended to ignore this bad omen and the terrible ache in his stomach. He ordered his men to take the militia into custody and started marching them to jail as his band played "The Star Spangled Banner."

As they entered the city, a huge crowd gathered to watch the spectacle, and things started to turn ugly. Cries of "Damn the Dutch!" and cheers for Jefferson Davis and the Confederacy rang through the air. Some angry citizens hurled stones and clots of mud at the Union soldiers. Stories differ on what happened next, but many agree that a man got pushed down in the confusion, pulled out a pistol, and shot a Home Guard soldier. The Home Guard units opened fire into the crowd, causing a massive stampede as the civilians fled. The air filled with the sharp smell of burnt gunpowder as both sides traded shots. By the time Lyon and his men made it back to their barracks, twenty-eight civilians lay dead on the streets behind them, including two women and a child. Two Union soldiers were killed and a few more wounded.

The Camp Jackson Massacre, as it came to be called, inflamed the rebel press. The state legislature, which had been waffling on the subject of secession, immediately gave Governor Jackson military powers to fight the Union in case it "invaded" Missouri. He made his own call for volunteers, not for the Union as Lincoln had requested, but for the Confederacy. Pro-Unionist legislators left in disgust to establish their own loyalist government, and for the rest of the war Missouri would have two governments and be on both sides of the Civil War.

The seizure of Camp Jackson polarized people's opinions. Blood had been shed on the streets of St. Louis, and Missourians now had to choose a side. For the next four years Missouri would be engulfed in a bloody civil war.

BLACK TROOPS
SHOW THEIR METTLE

1862

During the bloody years of the Civil War, Bates County, on the border with Kansas, was a safe haven for rebel guerrillas. Several bands operated in the area, using the thick woodland and scattered farms as a base for their raids across the state line from Missouri into pro-Union areas of Kansas. They were used to seeing Union troops marching through the countryside in search of them, but in October 1862 rebel scouts witnessed something nobody had ever seen before—a black regiment marching to battle under the banner of the United States Army.

They were the First Kansas Colored Volunteers, made up of free blacks from Kansas and runaway slaves from Missouri and Arkansas, organized by the fiery Kansas senator James Lane to compensate for a shortage of soldiers from his state. Many white people doubted blacks could make good soldiers, but Lane wanted to give them a chance. Besides, he had participated in some raids into Missouri himself and harbored a deep resentment against the rebels.

When a *New York Times* correspondent visited their camp a few weeks before they arrived in Bates County, he wrote:

> *[T]he aptitude of the men for acquiring the drill has already made their progress more than equal to any body of white men so new to the service. . . . The camp is a model of neatness and order, both officers and men having a great pride in its appearance. The most inveterate Negro hater who has yet visited it, has been constrained to commend the clean and orderly appearance of the equipment.*

Performing well in front of "inveterate Negro haters" must have been important to the new recruits. While preparing to battle the Confederate army, they already were battling prejudice. The soldiers knew anything less than perfection would be held up as proof of their inferiority.

The government didn't treat them fairly either. There were no black officers yet, and the pay was only $10 a month, while white soldiers received $13. This insult was compounded by the fact that they received no pay at all for several months.

On October 27, 1862, the First Kansas Colored Volunteers arrived at the farm of John Toothman, a prominent local rebel, near the Osage River in Missouri, amidst a rolling landscape of prairie grass and low mounds. The largest was Island Mound, a long, low hill overlooking the entire area. Toothman was already in jail, so the soldiers fortified the farm with logs and named it "Fort Africa."

For the Confederate guerrillas this was the realization of their worst fears. The Union had finally sent troops to occupy their homes. Rebels in the Civil War, especially in states like Missouri where citizens took both sides, ran a terrible risk. To fight for the Confederacy meant their property was forfeit, and Union troops often helped themselves to their valuables. Senator Lane himself had done his share of plundering, once making off with the carriage of a Missouri senator, which he gave to his wife as a present.

The rebels struck the next day, sniping at the sentries from long range. Once the rebels realized the black troops wouldn't be scared off, they decided on a more serious attack. On October 29 the Confederates under Colonel Jeremiah Cockrell set fire to the prairie grass near the fort and drove the sentries inside.

Union commander Colonel Henry Seaman peered through the thick smoke but couldn't tell how many rebels he faced, so he sent out a patrol led by a Cherokee named John Six-Killer. The patrol went too far, however, and became lost to view in the smoke. Seaman sent another patrol to join up with them.

This command proved fortunate, for shortly thereafter a force of Confederate cavalry came galloping out of the smoke at the scouts. Both sides opened fire, attracting more rebel cavalry to the fray. The Union men found themselves outnumbered and withdrew to the southern slope of Island Mound. The slope made it harder for the Confederates to charge, the best way for cavalry to break up an infantry formation, and this gave the Union troops a bit of an advantage. At times the fighting became hand-to-hand, with rebel cavalry slashing at the Union troops with sabers while the infantrymen stabbed the horsemen with bayonets. Seaman heard the firing and sent more troops, but for a time twenty-five Union men stood against more than two hundred rebel cavalry. The reinforcements from Fort Africa turned the tide of the battle, and the rebels retreated.

On the battlefield eight of the First Kansas Colored Volunteers lay dead, including John Six-Killer, and ten more wounded. Confederate losses are unclear, but estimates indicate about thirty killed and many more injured.

Tales of the skirmish made it into newspapers across the divided country. The fight hadn't accomplished much, and rebel bands operated out of Bates County for the rest of the war, but it was the first time an American black regiment saw combat. Their victory helped dispel doubts about the effectiveness of black troops and inspired other black regiments.

Over the next three years, the First Kansas Colored Volunteers fought battles in Arkansas, Kansas, and the Indian Territory, seeing more combat than any other black regiment in the war and having 156 men killed in action. It is unknown how many of these "Kansas" soldiers actually hailed from Missouri, but they made up a sizable portion of the volunteers. In 1864 their sacrifices earned them enough respect to get paid the same as white troops.

GENERAL PRICE'S INVASION OF MISSOURI

1864

The Civil War was going badly for the South. A Union blockade of Southern ports starved the Confederacy of trade and resources, and the Confederate army, although brave in the field, was steadily losing against a more numerous and better-equipped foe.

In Missouri, Southern sympathizers engaged in guerrilla raids across the state, but most of Missouri remained in Union hands. The Confederate state government was in exile far away in Marshall, Texas, while Missouri Confederate troops were stationed in Arkansas or east of the Mississippi.

The leader of Missouri Confederate troops in Arkansas was Major General Sterling Price, a slave owner and former governor, and he was determined to retake Missouri for the Confederacy.

In September 1864 he saw his chance. Because there had not been a major battle in Missouri for some time, many Union troops had transferred to the eastern campaigns, leaving the state protected mostly by poorly trained militias. Spread across the countryside, these militias guarded the railways and towns and tried to hunt down bush-whackers, as the Confederate guerrillas were called. Price gathered an army of twelve thousand men with the intention of taking St. Louis. While most of the men were mounted and included veterans such as Joseph Shelby's Iron Brigade and Major General John Marmaduke's division, about one-third of the army had no guns, and many were conscripts or deserters Shelby had rounded up that summer. The Confederate governor of Missouri, Thomas Reynolds, rode along in the hope of reinstating himself in the state capital of Jefferson City.

The force crossed into Missouri on September 19, ready to risk everything to take their state for the Confederacy. The Union commander of Missouri, Major General William Rosecrans, gathered the militias together and called for reinforcements from Illinois to protect St. Louis.

The rebels' first major battle was at the town of Pilot Knob, in the lead-rich Arcadia Valley. About a thousand Union soldiers were stationed in Fort Davidson just outside of town, and Price hoped to capture the fort and the large supply of weapons and ammunition stored there. His poorly armed men would need them if they hoped to take St. Louis.

As Shelby and his cavalry rode up the Iron Mountain Railroad, destroying tracks and bridges and cutting the region off from the outside world, Price's army surrounded the fort. The garrison was commanded by Thomas Ewing, who had authored the notorious Order Number 11. This decree was his way of getting rid of rebel sympathizers along the Kansas border. He forced everyone suspected of supporting the rebellion to leave their homes and depopulated the whole region. Looters and guerrillas swept in, creating such devastation that the area became known as the "Burnt District." Capturing this hated Northerner would be a good start to the rebels' campaign. On September 27, Price attacked.

The fort stood in an open, flat valley and was surrounded by a ditch and an earthen rampart. Waves of Price's men advanced on the earthworks, only to get cut down by withering musket fire. The fort's many cannons fired grapeshot, a packet of metal balls much like a shotgun shell, cutting bloody paths through the rebel ranks. But the Confederates pressed on, making it to the ditch, only to be fired on at point-blank range. The Union defenders hurled crude grenades down on the Confederates, adding to the slaughter and giving the rebels no choice but to retreat. More than a thousand of their compatriots lay dead or dying in the fields around the fort. Night fell on a grisly scene.

Ewing, however, did not want to face another day of fighting. During the attack the rebels had shelled Fort Davidson from the hills, and although his own artillery had driven them off, he feared they might try again. Also, he had lost about one-quarter of his men in the attack and the skirmishing of the previous two days. In the early hours before dawn, he marched his troops out of the fort and right past a Confederate camp. Apparently the rebels thought they were a friendly unit and didn't even bother to check. An hour later the Arcadia Valley lit up with a tremendous explosion as a slow-burning fuse ignited the magazine in the fort. Price had gained nothing.

But he had lost something vital—time. The days spent besieging Fort Davidson and chasing Ewing's force, which eventually got away, allowed Rosecrans to reinforce St. Louis. Price decided he couldn't take the city and headed for his secondary objective, Jefferson City.

The army marched across the state, looting the countryside for food and other supplies. In mid-October the rebels reached Jefferson City, only to find it protected by five forts. They looked longingly at the state capital, but remembered their previous experience with fortified positions and didn't dare attack. Although no one said the words, they began to realize that they were no longer campaigning but were in fact on the run.

The rebel force headed upriver to Boonville, a pro-Southern town, and gathered more than a thousand new recruits. A detachment of the army took Glasgow, where it seized a store of coats, guns, and horses; fresh supplies that helped raise morale. But with Price's ranks swollen with untrained volunteers and refugees, he moved slowly, and the Federals had time to gather. Coming up behind Price was a force of almost fourteen thousand sent by Rosecrans, while at Kansas City General Samuel Curtis commanded a similarly sized army. Most of Curtis's men, however, were Kansas militia who refused to fight in Missouri, so he was able to move only about two thousand men forward under the command of Major General James Blunt.

At the Little Blue River, Price almost surrounded Blunt's smaller force and made them retreat through Independence before taking up positions behind the Big Blue River. Luckily for the Union troops, they were joined by the Kansas militia, who, fearful of Kansas City being taken, decided to fight in Missouri after all.

Price now faced the danger of being caught between two large armies. On the morning of October 22, Shelby's Iron Brigade waded across the Big Blue and pushed the Federals back, capturing many Kansans in the process, but it was clear they had to keep moving before Rosecrans's large army caught up. Price ordered his men to move south. To cover his retreat, on October 23 he sent Shelby to attack Westport, just south of Kansas City. A fierce engagement ensued during which both sides suffered heavy losses before the Federals retreated. Meanwhile, Marmaduke tried to stop the Union troops from crossing the Big Blue. The fearless general had two horses shot from under him but held the line against a bigger force for several hours.

Price was able to get his men free of the noose. The Battle of Westport, the largest battle west of the Mississippi, was over.

But Price's campaign had one more long, deadly chapter before it could end. The Confederates entered Kansas pursued by Federal cavalry, who caught up with them at Mine Creek on October 25. In a short fight the Federals captured Marmaduke and about six hundred men. The bulk of the rebel army escaped, but in a disorderly and dispirited condition and without many of their supply wagons. Blunt caught up with them again near Newtonia. Once again Price was able to withdraw with his army intact, and his men continued their weary way south as the weather worsened and added to their misery with rain, sleet, and snow. Many deserted.

But the nightmare wasn't over yet. The men had run out of food and resorted to eating horses and mules. Smallpox and other diseases ravaged the ranks. Some soldiers, having no blankets and only ragged clothing, simply froze to death. In the beginning of December, Price made it back to Laynesport, Arkansas, with only a few thousand men.

In retrospect it seems doubtful that Price could have taken St. Louis, but his invasion managed to divert troops from the eastern campaigns and caused a wave of fear among Northern sympathizers in Missouri. The destruction of railways and supplies was a blow to the Union cause in the state, and Price's epic ride captured the imagination of the South. His army had traveled 1,434 miles and fought forty-three battles and skirmishes. Even if he and his brave men were not able to ride into St. Louis, they did ride into the history books.

OUTLAWS, LAWMEN,
AND OUTLAW LAWMEN

1872

The town of Joplin had too much of a good thing. The hotels were full of visitors, the population was booming, and local businesses were making more money than they ever had. The tinkling of pianos and loud drunken laughs echoed out of the saloons late into the night. Lead—useful for joints, sealing, roof tiles, bullets, and, unfortunately, water pipes—had been discovered in Joplin Creek. When news of the profitable ore spread, at first only a few prospectors from neighboring counties showed up to what was then a sleepy little hamlet in southwestern Missouri. There was plenty of lead in Missouri, and people weren't sure this would be a rich vein.

It was. Much of the lead lay so near the surface a miner could simply break the ground with a pickax and shovel it out. Soon miners were pouring in from all over the state, creating a Lead Rush much like the famous Gold Rush of California. A year earlier local settler John Cox had filed a plat for a town and named it Joplin, after a Methodist minister who had settled in the area. Like San Francisco,

Joplin sprang up almost overnight, and the cooperative and friendly early prospectors soon found themselves swamped by a horde of unruly and often dishonest men. These men gave their mines all sorts of wild names, such as Hello Dad, Get There, and Wild Rose. One prospector named his mine Sweet Relief because he was so relieved to finally find some lead and save himself from bankruptcy.

Within a year of its founding, Joplin boasted a post office, hotels, restaurants, and stores, but it had no law and no church. Worshippers gathered on Sundays at one of the town's five saloons, but for law enforcement, residents had to fend for themselves or ride seventeen miles to get the sheriff in Carthage. With money flowing out of the mines, plenty of unsavory characters gathered to "mine the miners."

By 1872 Joplin was becoming intolerable to decent folk as thieves, gamblers, con men, and madams ran local affairs. Miners fought one another over disputed claims or descended into drunken brawls over nothing at all. Gunmen practiced their aim on windows while drunks passed out on the sidewalks. The young town was rapidly descending into chaos—and something had to be done to halt the lawlessness.

Respectable citizens in Joplin and nearby Murphysburg formed Union City on March 14, 1872, but changed the name to Joplin the following year. By combining their towns they had enough resources to build a jail and hire a marshal, J. W. Lupton. Just a month before his appointment, Lupton had beaten up the worst of the local bullies, a violent man named "Dutch" Pete, who terrorized honest and dishonest citizens alike—thus proving himself to be the toughest man in town. This act gained Lupton the respect, or at least the fear, of everybody.

Unfortunately, Lupton may not have been all that honest himself, and he was certainly hot tempered. Although he restored order to the wild town, in 1874 some locals accused him of fining gamblers and prostitutes and keeping the money. Apparently his $100-a-month salary, while good for the time, wasn't enough to satisfy him. Lupton professed his innocence, but the town council didn't believe him, stripped him of his position, and named W. B. McCracken as his successor.

As the story goes, McCracken went to the jail for his first day of work but couldn't unlock it because he didn't have a key. McCracken tried to pick the lock and as he was fumbling with it, Lupton appeared with his set of keys and opened the door for him. McCracken thanked him, only to have Lupton shove him inside and lock the jail door behind him. McCracken screamed and hollered, demanding to be released. Being locked up in his own jail wasn't a good way to start his job as marshal.

Lupton just laughed and left him there. When McCracken realized he wasn't going to get out, he promised Lupton he would resign if he was released from his imprisonment. That was all Lupton wanted to hear, and he let McCracken out.

Apparently the town council was just as intimidated as McCracken had been because they didn't try to fire Lupton immediately. But the council finally decided enough was enough, and it appointed W. S. Norton to be marshal. Not taking any chances, Norton deputized two men and had them accompany him to the jail, where they unscrewed the hinges from the door. Norton then carried it to the local blacksmith to have it fitted with a new lock. He left the deputies to guard the jail in case Lupton decided to cause any trouble. Norton's suspicions proved correct. Lupton appeared at the jail with a pair of local toughs and beat up the two deputies.

Just as they finished off the deputies, Norton came back from the blacksmith's. Unlike McCracken, this new marshal wasn't going to be intimidated. He whipped out his Colt .45. Lupton did the same, but just before the two marshals were about to shoot it out in a very unpoliceman-like manner, the local judge who had come to see the excitement dove between them and stopped the fight.

The town council then got a writ from the court in Carthage to formally relieve Lupton of his job, but Lupton still had friends in low places. Supporters of the town council armed themselves and holed up in the jail and city hall as Lupton gathered a crowd of supporters, also armed. Eventually cooler heads prevailed and the mob dispersed.

The Carthage court then ruled that the Joplin town council hadn't ousted Lupton in the proper manner and that he was still marshal. He received all his back pay and, just to prove his point, got reelected marshal in October 1874, much to the chagrin of the town's more law-abiding citizens. He felt he had been vindicated, so from then on he put only criminals in jail, instead of marshals.

THE JAMES GANG ROBS A TRAIN

1874

As the *Little Rock Express* left St. Louis on January 3, the passengers settled in for the ride. Some gazed out the windows at the countryside, while others read newspapers or chatted together, sharing stories of what they would do once they made it to Arkansas. They expected it to be an uneventful, boring ride, but little did they know that Missouri's most notorious outlaws lay in wait for them—Frank and Jesse James.

When the Civil War broke out, Frank fought in the Confederate army and later joined the guerrilla band of notorious rebel William Quantrill. His younger brother Jesse stayed on the family farm until Union militiamen whipped him and nearly hanged his stepfather as suspected rebels. Thus began Jesse's lifelong hatred of Northerners. Soon he, too, joined the guerrillas. When the war ended, they and many other guerrillas decided they couldn't fit into the new society. The Confederacy had become a lost cause and the US government had labeled them and their fellow guerrillas criminals during the war, so criminals they would be.

The gang decided to rob the train at Gads Hill, Wayne County, a tiny railroad stop with a population of about fifteen. This sleepy little town was turned upside down when five hooded horsemen rode in. Brandishing shotguns and pistols, they rounded up the townsfolk. While obviously dangerous men, the outlaws had some compassion—they allowed the frightened citizens to build a bonfire to keep warm.

The masked men weren't so charitable to the storekeeper, however, and relieved him of several hundred dollars. Then they opened a switch so that the train would be forced onto a siding and unable to bypass the station even if the crew sensed trouble. One man stood on the platform while the others hid themselves.

When the train steamed into view, the man on the platform waved a red flag, something every railway man recognized as a signal to stop. The engineer braked, and the conductor leapt off the train to discover the cause of the commotion. Both must have been surprised when the train moved onto the siding. Just then the other outlaws came out of their hiding places, and in moments the crew faced five masked gunmen.

Two robbers pointed guns at the engineer and fireman and made them get off the engine, announcing that if anyone caused trouble they would be shot. By this point several passengers had come onto the platform, but the robbers ordered everyone back to their seats. Seeing the guns, everyone complied.

Everyone, that is, but express messenger Bill Wilson, whose job it was to guard the express mail and the substantial amount of money it contained. Gripping a pistol, he waited for his chance. The February 5 edition of the *St. Louis Dispatch* printed Wilson's testimony:

> *I fastened the door at my end of the car, and took a*
> *position facing the door. . . . I had waited but a short*

time when one of the robbers appeared at the door lead-
ing into my department. He had his hands filled with
registered letters. I pointed my pistol at him and told
him to "drop those letters," which he did instantly. At
this time two more robbers entered the car by the side
doors and, pointing their guns at me, told me to "drop
that pistol." I dropped it, or rather handed it to the one
that reached for it.

The man who had dropped the letters put a pistol
in my face and said, "You was going to shoot me, was
you? I've a notion to blow the top of your head off."

Luckily for Wilson, they made him unlock the safe instead. It didn't take long for the outlaws to clean out all the money contained in the letters inside. At this point Wilson, who seemed to have more backbone than brains, said to one of them, "I have always been in the habit of having people sign a receipt when I deliver them packages."

Fortunately the surprised outlaw had a sense of humor and, instead of giving Wilson a good thrashing, took the receipt book and signed "Robbed."

After looting the mail the outlaws turned their attentions on the passengers. The James Gang had a reputation for chivalry, not robbing women or the poor, and not harming anyone who didn't cause trouble. This reputation was exaggerated, however, as the robbery of the *Little Rock Express* would soon show.

As the gang made their way through the passenger compartment, they checked the hands of the men. If a passenger had the calluses of a workingman, they left him alone or only took small items like pocket money or tobacco. They even returned a gold watch to one of the crew when they learned it had been a present. If a man was well dressed with the soft palms of an office worker, they took everything.

They spared all the women except for one who had $400 in her purse. This proved a little too tempting, and the gang suspended their rule of not robbing women.

Nobody was hurt in the Gads Hill heist. But as the gang mounted up, what they didn't know was that this particular job would cost them dearly.

It's not clear how much money the gang got away with. Newspaper reports vary, but Wilson estimated the mail contained about $4,000, and the passengers lost a few hundred more, as well as some watches and other property.

As soon as the train made it to the next station, the crew telegraphed the news to the world. Locals formed a posse and headed out in pursuit, chasing the robbers through several counties before they fell behind and had to give up. The former guerrillas of the James Gang were experts at fighting and running in the brush, and no mere group of townspeople could ever catch them. Reports of their movements kept coming in, however, as everyone remained on the lookout for five armed riders, and they were traced all the way to St. Clair County before the trail went cold.

This route suggests one or more of the Younger brothers, who sometimes rode with the James Gang, took part in the robbery because they often hid out in St. Clair County. The James brothers, apparently, continued on to Clay County, where they holed up at their mother's house near Kearney.

The railroad company hired the Pinkerton National Detective Agency to apprehend the men responsible for the heist. Agent Joseph Whicher showed up at the James farm disguised as a farmhand looking for work, hoping to catch them unawares. The next day he was found dead by a road many miles away. Two more Pinkertons, Louis Lull and John Boyle, went after Jim and John Younger. The agents hired Edwin Daniels, a local, as their guide. As they scouted the area close to where the Youngers were hiding, the outlaws came riding up behind them. Boyle panicked and rode off, but the other two tried to talk their way out. The Youngers didn't believe their story about being in the area to buy cattle as they claimed, and so the outlaws disarmed them. Lull, thinking they would be killed, whipped out a hidden pistol and shot John Younger in the neck just as John shot him in the arm. Jim Younger drew his gun and killed Daniels as Lull rode off. Ignoring the blood pouring from his neck, John rode after Lull and gave him a mortal wound before slipping off his horse and out of this life.

Infuriated at the deaths of three of its agents, the Pinkerton agency took a terrible revenge. A few months after the shoot-out, an agent tossed a bomb into the Jameses' cabin, killing their eight-year-old half-brother Archie and wounding their mother. The Jameses and the Youngers paid a bloody price for robbing that train at Gads Hill.

The James brothers continued their life of crime across several states, but their careers came to an abrupt end on April 3, 1882, when a fellow gang member killed Jesse for the reward money. Frank turned himself in shortly thereafter, and a court found him not guilty of all charges. This surprising verdict might have been the result of a secret deal in which Frank promised never to rob again. True to his word, he lived a peaceful life until his death in 1915. In a statement to the *St. Louis Republican* on October 6, 1882, he confided that a career in crime "was a life of taut nerves, of night-riding and day-hiding, of constant listening for footfalls, crackling twigs, rustling leaves and creaking doors . . . of seeing Judas in the face of every friend."

CONNECTING THE
BOOTHEEL TO THE WORLD

1880

Louis Houck wanted to build a railroad. The German immigrant and Cape Girardeau lawyer looked around his quiet Mississippi River town and saw the world was passing it by. The steamboat trade that had made the town prosperous was dwindling in favor of the new railroads appearing all across the state and nation.

Nearly ten years earlier, local businessmen had formed the Cape Girardeau and State Line Railroad to connect the town with Delta, another town fifteen miles away and on the busy St. Louis–Iron Mountain line. The company cut a path through the southeastern Missouri swamp through to Delta and farther on toward the Arkansas state line. They had graded forty miles of line, making a firm, raised ridge of stones covered with soil, but they covered only two miles of the grading with track before a bad recession left the company bankrupt.

Houck thought he could do better. He believed he had more business sense, and what did it matter if he didn't know anything about building a railroad? He had read several books on the subject, and it didn't look that hard.

The main problem was money. Houck was a successful lawyer, but he wasn't rich, certainly not rich enough to finance the operation himself. But his wife, well, that was another matter. Dear old Mary came from one of the wealthiest families in the Bootheel, and her father had recently died, leaving her the family fortune. For days the family home of Elmwood, a grandiose mansion designed in the style of a Scottish castle, rang with Houck's strident German-accented English as he gave his wife the sales pitch of his life. The Cape Girardeau and State Line Railroad was broke, he said, but the financial company that owned the deeds wanted to put the decaying line to use. With some starting capital he could get to work and attract more investors, and once he connected Cape Girardeau to Delta and the main railway system, the sleepy Bootheel town would be part of a national network stretching from the Atlantic to the Pacific, and from Canada to Mexico. The region's agricultural produce and rich lumber resources could be sold to the world. Property values would rise, too—good news since both Houck and his wife owned large amounts of real estate. And if they found running a railroad not to their liking, they could always sell it to a bigger company for a large profit.

After much thought, Mary assented. Houck immediately hit up his rich friends for more loans and got to work.

Houck conferred with the finance company that held the railroad's mortgages. In a flourish of self-confidence, he promised to finish the line by January 1, 1881, and pay $6,000 for the deeds in exchange for all the old railroad's properties. Another line in the contract stated that if he didn't finish, the company would receive all of the track he had laid for free, and Houck would have to personally pay off thousands of dollars in loans.

This was in August, and Houck's new Cape Girardeau Railway Company had yet to lay a single foot of track, but that didn't worry the hardy German entrepreneur. According to his reading, his newly hired crew should be able to lay a mile of track a day. He'd be done before winter.

At this point the tracks of reality derailed Houck's locomotive of optimism. The line was graded, true, but in the steamy climate of southeastern Missouri, thick briars and trees had sprung up, creating a nearly impassable tangle along the entire route. His crew spent more time clearing a path than laying track. Many of his engineers and supervisors, sensing their boss's ignorance of engineering, had exaggerated their experience in their job interviews and ended up relying as much on guesswork as he did. The only people who really knew what they were doing were the black laborers, who had long experience cutting and laying wooden ties for other railway companies.

It didn't help that the men had no confidence whatsoever in his venture. The previous railway had failed even though it was run by qualified personnel, and the fact that he rarely paid on time didn't inspire their confidence in his financial ability either.

Houck's cost-cutting measures affected the quality of the work, too. The Iron Mountain railroad sold him a shipment of faulty ties and instead of buying new ones, he picked out the most usable ties and had his men spread them farther apart, making the track on top of them shaky and unstable.

The "train" he purchased for his new line wasn't any better. Buying an old castoff locomotive and three flatcars from another railroad company, Houck discovered that he could keep the train on the rickety track only if he ran it backward. The caboose liked to jump the line, too, but Houck had nobody to blame for that because he had built it himself.

By early December the crew had laid only four miles of track. With the deadline looming less than a month away, and the grading covered in snowdrifts from a sudden storm, they still had to complete more than half the distance. Instead of one mile a day as his books told him, Houck's crew had managed only one mile a month.

But Houck wasn't a quitter. He hired more men and worked beside them seven days a week. At Mary's suggestion he offered them a $100 bonus if they made it another four miles in the next ten days.

The crew set to work with renewed energy, working through a bitter cold snap and making the goal. Then they offered Houck a counterproposal—if they finished by Christmas, would he give them another $100 bonus?

Houck agreed. The thrifty lawyer had learned that you have to spend money to make money.

The crew redoubled its efforts, but exhaustion, continuing bad weather, and poor materials, which often had to be fixed or thrown away and replaced, slowed the work until it became obvious they wouldn't get done by the holidays. Desperate, Houck promised them the bonus anyway as long as they finished by the New Year's deadline. If he didn't get it done, he, and possibly Mary, would face financial ruin.

On the last day of 1880, they still had half a mile to go to connect to the old Cape Girardeau line. At the beginning of the project, it would have taken two weeks to complete the distance, but now the crew worked as an efficient machine and felt confident of making it if they worked right until midnight. Mary wisely suggested offering the men another day's wages if they worked through the night. Not only did the project require that extra time, but she also worried that the men might go into town for some New Year's drinking and not come back.

At 11:00 p.m. the men raised a loud cheer into the Missouri night. They hadn't started drinking as Mary feared; they had something even better to celebrate. The line was finished! Victorious, they clambered on board the old locomotive and reversed into Cape Girardeau at 2:00 a.m. on January 1, 1881. Louis Houck had his railroad.

Despite his rocky start, Houck decided that railroads were his calling and built an additional five hundred miles of track over the next forty years. His work helped bring prosperity to himself and the once-quiet region as he connected it with an ever-quickening world.

CHAMPION CYCLISTS RACE
IN CLARKSVILLE

1887

It was 9:00 a.m. on May 23, 1887. A thick early morning mist had disappeared, and the sun had begun to shine. It promised to be a warm, pleasant day, and for the expectant crowd lined up along the Belt Road near Clarksville, it also promised to be an exciting one. They'd come to see a championship race on that newfangled contraption—the bicycle.

If a modern person could go back in time, they'd see a very different bicycle race than they were used to. Bicycles back then were of the "Ordinary" type, with the front wheel far bigger than the back. The front wheel could be up to sixty inches in diameter while the back could be as little as twelve. This increased speed until the invention of chain drives and sprocket gears that same decade made the giant front wheel unnecessary.

The Ordinary bicycle was built of cast iron with solid rubber tires. This made the bicycle heavy, and the giant wheel made it unstable. It didn't help that most roads at the time were unpaved. Hitting a pothole or a rock could send the rider into a painful "header." If the rider got tangled in the spokes, a header could be disastrous, and the Ordinary soon earned the nickname "Man Slicer."

They were also hard to get started. On a modern bicycle the rider can simply push off with one foot. Since an Ordinary was often as tall as the man riding one, that was impossible. To mount the tallest machines, the cyclist had to step up on a platform of some kind. For the Clarksville race, each man had someone behind him ready to give him a push.

Experiments were still the norm in cycling, and one of the contestants came to the race with a tricycle to see if he could beat his two-wheeled rivals.

Most of the crowd gathered that day had probably never ridden a bicycle, and some may not have even seen one before. The first bicycles had appeared in St. Louis only nine years before and were still considered novelties in 1887. They were catching on, however, and St. Louis was a center for the new sport with several cycling clubs.

One of them was the local chapter of the League of American Wheelmen, who managed to get St. Louis picked as the site for the eighth annual meet in 1887. Besides club business, socializing, and of course outings on their bicycles, there would be the usual race—a "century" of a hundred miles.

The site picked for the race was a loop of roads called the Belt Road that started and ended at Clarksville. The town was easily accessible by steamboat from St. Louis, and the roads on the loop were mostly graveled. Some even had a covering of macadam. There were still stretches of dirt road, however, and enough potholes, mud slicks, tight curves, and steep hills to keep things interesting.

Delegates from clubs all across the nation started appearing in St. Louis on May 19. The mood was festive, and everyone ate, drank, danced, and sang bicycle songs late into the night. Some three hundred cyclists treated St. Louis to a parade.

After a few days all the delegates had gathered and headed down to Clarksville on trains and a specially commissioned steamer. There had been some hard rain, and they worried about the conditions of the road.

The contestants were a veritable *Who's Who* of early American cycling. William Rhodes of Boston was the favorite. Robert Neilson, also of Boston, was on his team. Teams in those days were sponsored by bicycle manufacturers as a way to promote the sport and advertise their machines. Rhodes and Neilson rode for the Overman Company, which sold the Victor bicycle, a tall version that could measure up to sixty inches high.

Another team used the Star, a type of Ordinary that had the big wheel at the back and the small wheel in front. These eliminated the danger of headers but added a new one: If the cyclist climbed an especially steep hill, sometimes the Star could flip backward. Charles Frazier of Smithville, New Jersey; A. McCurdy of Lynn, Massachusetts; and John Brooks of Pennsylvania represented this team. Frazier was competing with a handicap—on a test run around the track he was descending a steep hill at top speed when his bicycle broke. One of the sharp metal pieces gouged his knee. Grimacing with pain, he decided to compete anyway. Everyone except Rhodes had taken tumbles in recent days, a testimony to how dangerous their sport could be.

H. G. Crocker of Boston rode a fifty-eight-inch Columbia. Stillman Whittaker hailed from Chicago and was tipped as a likely winner because he was the current record holder for twenty- and hundred-mile races. He had some drawbacks, however. He had been recovering from a fall and rode a Champion, a heavy brand of Ordinary weighing forty-two pounds, about ten more than any other bicycle in the race.

Samuel Hollingsworth of Rushville, Indiana, had a Columbia. Charles Ashinger of Omaha rode a Champion. L. D. Munger of Detroit rode a Quadrant tricycle.

As the racers perched atop their tall bicycles, they could hear the cheers of the crowd. They checked the sky nervously but saw no sign the previous day's rain would return. In fact, it looked like heat would be more of a problem. The master of ceremonies raised his starter pistol. Each pusher braced one leg behind the other. At the crack of the pistol they all heaved on the bicycles, giving each racer the momentum to make a quick start up the incline at the beginning of the route. The crowd ran after them cheering.

At first Frazier kept ahead. Soon Crocker sped into first place, only for Frazier to pass him six miles down the road. The others jockeyed for position, too, but this was more psychological than tactical. They had five laps on the course for a total of a hundred miles. There would be plenty of chances to make it to first place—or last.

Soon the racers found their pace. The sun rose higher. By the end of the first lap they were all sweating profusely. Rhodes, Neilson, and Crocker stayed in the lead for the first two laps. Whittaker was getting overheated as he pedaled on his heavy machine and lagged behind in fourth place. His bicycle broke down on the second lap. He was given a replacement and managed to finish that lap at fourth place, followed by McCurdy three minutes later. Ashinger came near the back on this lap and soon dropped out of the race. Munger trailed far behind on his tricycle.

Now the heat was really beating down. Rhodes nearly fainted. Neilson, perhaps dizzy from the heat, took a header and cut up his face. He gamely picked himself up and regained his position.

The third lap ended with Rhodes, Neilson, and Crocker all still in a group in the lead. McCurdy was at fourth position more than twenty minutes behind them. Just as he finished the third lap, he hit a rock and fell over. His trainer rushed to get him back on his bicycle, but the accident had taken the fight out of him. He soon quit.

The race had eliminated two more cyclists. Brooks gave up shortly after completing the second lap, and Frazier's knee got so bad that he gave up halfway through the third lap.

It was now mid afternoon, and the sun was merciless. Rhodes and Neilson finished the fourth lap together with Crocker two minutes behind them. Farmers lined the racecourse offering water and milk. Rhodes grabbed a dipper full of water without stopping, took a sip, and discarded it, only for it to get caught in his spokes sending him into a header. Rhodes leapt back up on his bike and soon regained the lead with Neilson.

Crocker had worse luck. One of his supporters told a farmer to splash him with a bucket of water, but the bucket slipped through the man's fingers and smacked into Crocker's head, bowling him over. He was helped back on his machine and sent on his way before anyone told him what had happened.

Three thousand people had gathered at the finish line by the Clarksville paper mill, and a band was playing as they waited for the winners.

The two leaders turned a corner and came into sight, with Rhodes just ahead of Neilson. The crowd cheered Rhodes, their favorite, then gasped as Neilson pedaled like mad and shot past him. It was now Rhodes's turn to pick up the pace, but Neilson had more energy left and widened the lead to finish first, a hundred feet ahead of Rhodes. Neilson had raced a primitive bicycle a hundred miles over bad conditions in six hours, forty-six minutes, and twenty-seven seconds. Rhodes passed the finish line a few seconds later. The recorded time shows he finished twenty-four seconds after Neilson, but this doesn't seem correct if he was only a hundred feet behind. Coming in third was Crocker, five minutes after Neilson.

Half an hour later Whittaker and Hollingsworth rode into view. They were right alongside one another when disaster struck.

Whittaker put on a burst of speed only to have several spokes fall out of his wheel. He swerved. Hollingsworth took advantage of Whittaker's bad luck and raced across the finish line ahead of him.

Last but not least came Munger, puffing along on his tricycle and finishing with a time of ten hours and four minutes. While he had failed to prove the tricycle's superiority over the bicycle, he could console himself that he had broken the American tricycle record for a hundred-mile race.

The race made national news, yet the days of the Ordinary were numbered. Within a few years bicycles with gears and evenly sized pneumatic tires would take over the roads. They proved to be faster, more comfortable, and far safer. They also changed the bicycle from a curio into something found in almost every home.

THE "KANSAS CYCLONE" DESCENDS ON MISSOURI

1901

One afternoon, a group of men stood smoking in Union Station, St. Louis, when they were suddenly interrupted by an imposing middle-aged woman outfitted in a conservative black dress, a black bonnet, and matching scarf. A full six feet tall and rather burly, she scowled at them and shouted, "I want all you hellions to quit puffing that hell-fume into God's clean air!" as she knocked cigars and cigarettes out of their astonished mouths.

Their uninvited companion had a crowd of reporters around her, and in another moment the men recognized her—it was Carry Nation, an outspoken critic of alcohol, smoking, and a host of other societal ills ranging from nude art to feather hats.

The smokers didn't know what to do. If it had been a man who had confronted them, then a fistfight would have been in order, but a woman? They could do little but grumble and sneak off to smoke somewhere else.

Nation had made a name for herself by smashing up saloons in Kansas. That state was theoretically "dry," but saloons operated openly, paying a fine each month to stay in business. Most people just shrugged their shoulders and let it happen, but not Carry Nation. Her beloved first husband had gone to an early grave because of alcoholism, and a stint as an evangelist to prisoners convinced her that it led to many other sins besides.

At that moment Nation was on a speaking tour for the temperance movement, which sought to ban alcohol nationwide. She raised money by selling books, photos of herself, and little hatchets, symbolizing her weapon of choice against saloons. The temperance movement was part of a growing push for women's rights, and many early female activists focused on alcohol because they felt it led to broken homes, abandoned and abused women, and unwanted pregnancies. Nation suffered beatings and arrests on numerous occasions but remained steadfast in her fight.

Eager for a good story, the reporters told her of a saloon nearby named after her. She stormed out of the train station, and the reporters led her to the city's Tenderloin district, a poor, crime-ridden area infamous for its cheap drinking dens. A curious crowd followed. Soon they stopped at the saloon of Joseph Sauerburger at 1616 Market Street. A big sign above the door read NATION LIQUOR STORE, with a painting of a hatchet over it.

"You take that sign down before I come back to this town, my man," she shouted at the proprietor, "or I'll use a little hatchetation on you!"

Sauerburger didn't need to ask what "hatchetation" meant. While the word could only be found in one dictionary, the one in Carry Nation's head, everyone knew it meant the destruction of a saloon by a very determined woman wielding a hatchet. The saloon owner put his hand on the grip of the revolver sticking out of his pocket and demanded she leave. She held her ground for a while, lecturing a young man drinking a beer at the bar that he would surely go to hell, and then she was gone, off on a train to Cincinnati to make a speech against that city's red-light district.

St. Louis had just been visited by what everyone called the "Kansas Cyclone." But although Carry Nation resided in Kansas, she had lived near Belton, Missouri, for many years and made frequent visits to Missouri.

Soon she was back in St. Louis to check on Sauerburger, and a large crowd followed her to the saloon. Finding the sign still in place, she grabbed a hatchet out of her bag and ran inside. With a sweep of her arm, she swung her weapon across the bar and took off every bottle and glass there.

This time Sauerburger drew his pistol. Nation retreated to the street as the drinkers laughed and shouted at her.

"God will smite you, you rummies!" she cried, shaking her fist at them. She then proceeded to another bar, where she sang a temperance song. The police eventually showed up and put her on the first train out of town.

On April 15 she appeared in Kansas City, primarily to visit her brother, but also to convince the citizens of the error of their ways. In an impromptu speech on the street, she said she didn't have any hard feelings for saloon owners. "I don't hate them but I hate the stuff they sell—the vile stuff that destroys both them and the men who buy it off them. There has never been a stroke of my hatchet that was not propelled by love for these men."

It may seem odd to help someone by smashing up his business, but Carry Nation meant what she said. She never got over the disappointment of her first love, the man who once seemed so wonderful but became so pathetic when he stumbled home drunk night after night. She wanted to save people from destroying themselves, and ruining a bar was far better than ruining a life.

So many people gathered during her speech that the police intervened and arrested her for blocking traffic. When taken to the jail, where bailiffs and prisoners puffed away on cigarettes, she had a chance to extol another of her causes.

"This is a regular hell hole," she said. "You could cut this smoke with a knife. You men who like to smoke so well will get plenty of it some day."

At her trial she claimed she had merely been waiting for a street-car. The arresting officer disagreed, saying he had counted eleven streetcars pass by without her boarding any, at which point Nation jumped up and called him a liar. That outburst got a $500 fine from the judge, who said she didn't have to pay if she got out of town that same day. Soon she was back across the state line.

Although many people then and now laugh at Carry Nation's adventures and are tempted to write her off as insane, she was in deadly earnest about her cause. Women in those days couldn't vote and had no say in civic affairs. With women being ignored and shoved aside, it's understandable that a strong-willed woman such as Nation would overcompensate. She once told a reporter, "The vote is the best hatchet. If I could vote, I wouldn't smash anymore." She also knew her tirades would get into the newspapers. In an age of reformers, nobody could grab a headline like she could.

Partly due to Nation's efforts, the temperance movement gained momentum in the early years of the twentieth century until the passage of the Eighteenth Amendment to the Constitution, which banned the use of alcohol nationwide in 1920. That same year saw the passage of the Nineteenth Amendment, giving women the right to vote. Sadly, Nation did not live to see her dreams come true. She died in 1911 and is buried in Belton.

THE TOUGHEST MARATHON
IN HISTORY

1904

The famous St. Louis World's Fair of 1904 showcased marvelous exhibitions of science, technology, art, and culture from dozens of countries and all of the United States, but overshadowed another important event in St. Louis. As fairgoers marveled at the fantastic displays and strolled wide avenues of the fairgrounds, the press paid less attention to what would soon become the world's most popular sporting celebration—the Olympics, which were being held in St. Louis that same year.

Despite a temperature of 90 degrees in the shade, ten thousand spectators packed Francis Field to watch the marathon. The thirty-two runners were a varied lot. Seventeen were Americans, including several recent immigrants such as Albert Corey, originally from France, and Thomas Hicks, who had been born in England. One of the more experienced runners, A. L. Newton, had been born in the United States. Newton had competed in the 1900 Paris Olympic marathon, and many believed he had the best chance of winning.

Eleven Greeks represented their country in the race, but none of them had any training as runners. Three South Africans competed, including two members of the Tswana people, named Len Taunyane and Jan Mashiani, called "Lentauw and Yamasini" by newspaper reporters and Olympic officials who couldn't figure out how to pronounce their names. The two students were the first black Africans ever to compete in the Olympics. The most colorful competitor had to be Felix Carvajal of Cuba, a mailman who trained by running his route. He even ran the length of Cuba to prove his fitness. Getting to the games had been a bit of a marathon in itself after he lost all his money in a craps game in New Orleans.

The crack of the starter pistol sent the athletes around the track and out of the stadium as the crowd roared encouragement. Once on the road, the runners began to spread out and set their paces. The sun hammered down on them. Olympic officials sped past in automobiles, sending up thick clouds of dust that often left the runners doubled over, hacking like lifelong smokers. One of the only sources of water along the route was a well near the halfway point. It couldn't have been very clean, because many of the athletes ended up with diarrhea or stomach cramps, not something a runner needs when competing in a marathon.

Sharp stones littered the route threatening to sprain or break an ankle, and the sun seemed to get hotter and hotter. People began to drop out. One US runner, William Garcia, swallowed so much dust that it caused his stomach to hemorrhage. He collapsed eight miles from the finish line and nearly died.

Under the blinding heat the English immigrant, Hicks, suffered terribly. A little more than halfway through, he looked ready to fall over. He begged the officials for some water, but they said no. Instead they sponged his mouth out, which at least gave a temporary respite from the dust that caked his tongue and palate. When he was seven miles from the finish line, he again looked close to collapse, and the officials gave him an egg white and some sulfate of strychnine, better known as rat poison. Why they thought this would relieve his suffering is a bit of a mystery, but it seemed to help, and he kept on going.

Carvajal was keeping a good pace. Being from Cuba, he was used to the heat, but he seemed more interested in the crowd than the race and frequently stopped to practice his English with the fans. At one point he approached an official's vehicle and asked for some peaches the official had in a basket. When the man said no, Carvajal grabbed a couple and ran off down the road, eating them as he went.

Corey and Newton were still in the race, as were Taunyane and Mashiani. Taunyane kept good time, but a huge angry dog charged at him and chased him almost a mile off course before the runner could shake it and get back into the race.

Meanwhile, the only thing keeping Hicks going was his lead position. If he could just maintain speed, he might win the gold. But at four miles from the finish line, he couldn't take any more and decided to lie down for a rest. The officials nearby knew that if he did that he'd never finish the race and convinced him to keep moving. Hicks slowed to a walk. Just then Fred Lorz of New York passed him. Hicks looked despondent and slowed almost to a stop.

Lorz entered the stadium and ran across the finish line. He barely looked winded, and none of the other runners had even come into view. The crowd cheered his easy victory, but it turned out that an official had caught him taking a car ride and had disqualified him on the spot. Apparently thinking he could still fool everybody, Lorz had the driver drop him off five miles from the finish line and ran the rest of the way. When the official returned to the stadium and spread the word, Lorz claimed it had been just a joke, but the judges weren't laughing and disqualified him.

The officials driving alongside Hicks gave him the good news. If he could just keep going, he could still win. But Hicks looked as though he would faint at any moment, and the steep hills near the end of the course almost stopped him. The officials gave him more strychnine, two more egg whites, and a sip of brandy. Now thoroughly poisoned as well as exhausted and dehydrated, he began to hallucinate that he still had twenty miles to go and ranted about how he was going to have a nice meal once he got there. With some more doses of brandy and egg white, he finally staggered across the finish line. He completed the distance in three hours, twenty-eight minutes, and fifty-three seconds, a good time considering the conditions. One observer said he looked like "one of the most tired athletes that ever wore a shoe."

Not long after, Corey panted his way into the stadium to win the silver, and Newton followed him to take the bronze. Carvajal came in fourth, and many believed that if had taken the race more seriously, he might have come in first. The two Tswana, Taunyane and Mashiani, placed ninth and twelfth, but if Taunyane hadn't been attacked by that dog, he would have done better. In all, only fourteen of the runners made it back to the stadium. Of the eleven Greeks who ran the marathon, four finished, with one coming in fifth. Considering their lack of training and the brutal conditions, it's a testament to their determination that any of them finished at all. Every single one of the runners who had completed the race honestly could be proud of besting such an endurance test, and their accomplishment should be remembered as much as the World's Fair.

While the marathon was full of drama, the rest of the 1904 Olympics proved quite eventful as well. This was the first Olympics to award gold, silver, and bronze medals and the first to have black African athletes, and a number of records were broken. One of the stars of the competition was US gymnast George Eyser, who won three golds, two silvers, and a bronze, despite having a wooden leg.

But even stranger than Eyser's accomplishments was the marathon, which to spectators must have seemed something out of the funny pages of the Sunday paper.

JOSEPH FOLK CLEANS UP MISSOURI

1905

By the dawn of the twentieth century, Missourians held their prosperous state in high esteem, but there were many problems people couldn't ignore. Corruption infected all levels of government and business. If, for example, a construction company wanted to win a contract to build a new streetcar line, a stack of money placed in the hands of the committee responsible for awarding the contract would ensure the deal went through—unless, of course, another contractor gave a bigger bribe. A few people got rich while little was done to improve rural roads, clear the cities of pollution and uncollected garbage, or rid the streets of crime.

Elections weren't any better. Politicians would get people to vote more than once, or they would simply fill out ballots themselves while throwing out those of their opponents. Graveyards became important voting districts as the dead turned out in record numbers. Political parties were often led by a "boss" who organized the rigging of elections to get his favored candidates elected. These candidates would then turn around and give contracts to the boss's businesses.

The boss in St. Louis was Ed Butler. He led the Democratic Party to victory in a number of rigged elections but happily made deals with Republicans if the GOP's Election Day trickery got the better of him. Butler and his party helped get a lawyer named Joseph Folk elected as circuit attorney for St. Louis. In his campaign Folk promised to rid the city of corruption, but Butler and his friends assumed that Folk meant *Republican* corruption. They soon got a nasty surprise.

Folk uncovered electoral fraud in both parties. Powerful Democrats warned him to behave, but he brought Ed Butler himself to trial, accusing him of bribing health officials to award one of his own companies the contract for garbage removal. The trial had to be moved to Boone County for fear the powerful boss would bribe or intimidate a St. Louis jury. Butler dressed as a farmer to impress the rural court, but it didn't work and they found him guilty. Butler eventually got the case overturned in the Supreme Court, where he had friends and Folk had enemies, but his reputation was ruined. Not even corrupt politicians wanted to align themselves with a known criminal.

This case set the tone for Folk's career. He would go after corruption wherever he saw it, bring the guilty party to court, and the case would be thrown out on appeal. Nonetheless, he managed to ruin the careers of a lot of corrupt politicians and businessmen just by bringing them to trial. His greatest victory came when he proved that Lieutenant Governor John Adams Lee had taken and given bribes for the Royal Baking Company to ensure their monopoly in the state. Lee had no choice but to resign. Lee was a Democrat, and from then on Folk had no hope of any support from his own party.

The system proved too corrupt for Folk's one-man crusade, but he gained a huge amount of popularity. People began to see the system could be challenged, and his support in St. Louis and the rest of the state grew, becoming part of a nationwide movement called Progressivism. Progressives believed that an open, honest government could bring reforms to society and improve people's lives. Folk decided to run for governor so he could have a better chance to make a difference.

But many newspaper editors, friends of the powerful people Folk had hurt, wrote scathing editorials about him. Some of his other enemies tried to fight him in the courts and state legislature. He was even told his crusade might endanger his health in a very sudden and unpleasant way.

Nonetheless, he was beginning to receive national recognition, and influential magazines and newspapers in other states championed his cause. This made him immune to any serious threat on his life. He also turned out to be a sharp campaigner, coming up with the slogan of the "Missouri Idea," in which good old Missouri values would clean out the state government and lead the way to national reform. This played well with voters sick of the way things had been going. Folk won the election easily, becoming governor in 1905.

"Holy Joe," as both his friends and his enemies called him, still had a fight ahead. His own party now hated him, and the Republicans had won all the other important offices. He tried to pass a number of reforms aimed at making government more honest, transparent, and democratic, but the state legislature defeated him again and again.

Folk did win a few victories. He passed laws allowing citizens the right to petition for bills to be put on a popular referendum, thus giving the people the opportunity to come up with new laws. He also passed a law allowing popular recall—a petition to have a special election to determine whether an unpopular politician should stay in office. These reforms, now considered an essential part of a democratic government, were considered radical at the time.

He also helped the career of another Progressive reformer, Herbert Hadley, who despite being a Republican served as Folk's attorney general. Hadley went after Standard Oil of New Jersey, owned by John D. Rockefeller, because the company operated an illegal monopoly in the state. When Rockefeller was called to testify, the millionaire temporarily fled the country. This encouraged other states to join in the effort, and soon Standard Oil lost its monopoly.

Hadley took over as governor in 1909. In that same election Progressives gained numerous seats in the state legislature, where they passed laws to create bipartisan election boards to fight corruption. Hadley safeguarded the state's food supply by setting up the office of dairy commissioner, food and drug commissioner, and game and fish commissioner. He also reformed the state's primitive prisons by installing showers, improving the food, and teaching job skills. But it had been Joseph Folk who had led the way for these reforms. Because of Folk's bravery in standing up to corruption in his own party, Missouri became a better and more democratic place to live.

FIRE AT THE CAPITOL!

1911

As First Lady Agnes Lee Hadley sat at her desk in the governor's mansion in Jefferson City on the Sunday evening of February 5, she heard a thunderstorm roll overhead. She was startled by a loud crack of thunder so close by that at first she thought it had hit her home. A short time later she looked out the window and saw a tongue of flame flickering from the dome of the Capitol building next door. The lightning had hit not the governor's mansion, but the Capitol, and flames lit up the darkness.

The Capitol had been built to replace Jefferson City's first Capitol, which had burned to the ground in 1837. In 1911 the building sported a 185-foot dome of pinewood sheathed in metal. The dome had lightning rods but they proved inadequate for the task.

All four of the city's volunteer fire brigades rushed to the scene. Governor Herbert Hadley ran to the Capitol building and, seeing that the flames were near the top of dome, realized the fire crews needed help. He hurried back to the mansion and called the local National Guard unit, the fire department of the nearby Lincoln Institute, the railroad company, and even the city's prison warden, who arrived with a dozen convicts to join the growing throng of people eager to save Missouri's center of government.

Despite all this help, the firefighters faced a serious problem. Their hoses didn't have enough pressure to reach the dome, so they entered the building and climbed onto the roofs of the Senate and House chambers on either side. But still they couldn't fight the blaze because of the building's architecture—the metal sheathing on the dome actually kept water from reaching the burning wood inside.

Firefighters finally got inside the dome, but their weak hoses could barely spurt a trickle of water. Soon they had to retreat as portions of the dome broke free and hurtled down like flaming meteors. At 8:30 p.m. the dome collapsed, sending a pile of burning wreckage onto the floor of the rotunda. Other fragments landed on the roof of the House of Representatives and set it on fire. The roofs of both wings of the Capitol were of the same pine that caught fire so easily in the dome, and much of the building's interior was wooden as well.

As it became increasingly obvious that the firefighters were losing the battle, the focus shifted to salvaging the irreplaceable records inside. The convicts, members of the General Assembly, and many locals ran in and scooped up as many papers as they could carry. Missourians of all backgrounds worked together in the coiling smoke, their heads covered with buckets or baskets to protect them from falling debris as they staggered under armloads of documents. Their bravery and teamwork saved virtually all of the state's records just in time: At 9:10 p.m. the roof of the House of Representatives collapsed, setting the second floor of that entire wing on fire.

Just before midnight the Sedalia Fire Company No. 2 arrived on a train loaded with the company's steam engine pump, one of the finest fire engines of its time. Although the Capitol was a mass of flames at this point, the extra water pressure proved vital in containing the blaze and keeping it from overcoming the building's fireproof bank vault, which contained hundreds of thousands of dollars in cash and state bonds.

At 4:00 a.m. another tragedy struck as the water main broke. No one is sure why it failed—perhaps some debris fell on a hose and backed up the water, or perhaps the system just became overworked. Regardless of the cause, the firefighters' efforts came to an abrupt halt. The main couldn't be fixed until Tuesday morning, and once it was they glumly hosed down the smoldering ruins and set about sifting through the rubble. They found that the fireproof vault had protected the money inside, but while the state's savings were untouched, the rest of the building was gutted.

Amazingly, no one was seriously injured. A few people suffered from scratches and smoke inhalation, but they quickly recovered. The convicts received a pardon for their role in saving the archives.

The Capitol lay in ruins, and now the citizens of Missouri would require a new seat of government. While the old structure had been an imposing edifice, there had been many complaints that the building was too old and small. Editorials had been calling for a new Capitol for at least a decade, and now they got their wish. The next building would be more grandiose and would reflect Missouri's prominent role in the nation.

The new state Capitol opened in October 1917 and still serves Missourians today. The building echoes the old in that it has two large wings flanking a central rotunda and high dome. The Capitol has three hundred thousand square feet of space, six times that of the previous structure, and is built of steel, concrete, and marble, making it much more fire resistant. It seems that the architects learned from bitter experience and created a building that will stand for generations to come.

THE GOLDEN LANE

1916

On June 14, 1916, St. Louis was a beehive of political activity. The National Democratic Convention was meeting to determine the party's platform for the upcoming election, and delegates from every state had gathered in the city as citizens welcomed them by hanging flags and putting up red, white, and blue bunting on their shops and homes. Missourians of both political parties knew this would be an important day. Democratic president Woodrow Wilson was running for reelection, and the delegates met in the convention hall to discuss the issues, mainly the debate over banning alcohol and whether to participate in the war in Europe. What most delegates weren't discussing was the rising call for women's suffrage—giving women the right to vote. The delegates were all men, and since women couldn't vote, they really didn't need to worry about what women thought.

That was about to change.

As the delegates left the meeting hall that afternoon, they were stunned by a remarkable sight. Both sides of the street were lined by a large crowd of women, each of whom wore a long white dress and held a yellow parasol. Each also wore a yellow sash emblazoned with the words "Votes for Women."

Some of the delegates jeered, while others looked straight ahead and tried to ignore the spectacle, but the more sympathetic men smiled and nodded their approval. The catcalls of those against the cause of women's suffrage soon died down as the delegates continued down the road. There seemed to be no end to the suffragettes, as women agitating for the vote were then called. Even more unnerving was that the protesters kept completely silent.

For block after block the delegates passed through a gauntlet of silent, watchful women. The "Golden Lane," as the press dubbed it, stretched for ten city blocks. As the delegates returned to their hotels or to restaurants to get their dinner, they couldn't escape the sight of thousands of women demanding their place in the democratic process.

The protest was the idea of Missouri suffragette Emily Newell Blair, who had been born in 1877 in Joplin to a prosperous family. When Emily was a child, her father had encouraged her education beyond that of most girls of that era—so much so that by the age of ten she was helping process deeds for her father, who was the Jasper County recorder. She then went on to college, but her hopes for completing her education were dashed when her father died after her first year at school. Her mother took over the family's mortgage loan business, and Emily had to return home to take care of the house and her younger siblings. She married in 1900, had two children, and settled down to what looked to be a normal upper-middle-class life.

Blair had long been active in a debating club and delighted in arguing about politics. A male opponent who was on the receiving end of one of her particularly strong arguments told her she had a "man's mind." In her autobiography she wrote that she felt flattered, but the comment also raised some questions. Why did an inquiring, forceful mind have to be a "man's mind"? Couldn't a woman's mind be that way, too?

Blair concentrated her efforts on writing, making a steady income by selling articles and short stories to prominent magazines such as *Cosmopolitan* and *Ladies' Home Journal.* She joined with several other writers to found the Missouri Women's Press Association, and got her first introduction to active politics when she became the editor of a new suffrage magazine called *The Missouri Woman.*

At the National Democratic Convention in St. Louis, Blair gathered thousands of women from across Missouri and other states. Rich women arrived by train from New York and Boston, while farmers' wives from the rural counties of Missouri joined factory workers from Kansas City and Chicago on the road to St. Louis. They represented all religions and social classes, and although they had differing views on virtually every subject, they were united in the belief that women should have their say in politics.

The women had put on an impressive display, but Blair worried she had been too ambitious in her protest. The "Golden Lane" covered such a large area that even the huge crowd of suffragettes couldn't line all the streets. There were wide gaps in the line, and although Blair originally wanted the line to be two women deep, in most places it was only one woman deep. Would the Democratic delegates see this as a sign of weakness and dismiss their cause?

The *St. Louis Post-Dispatch* seemed a bit dismissive when it called the suffragettes an "optimistic little army" and buried the story on page four. But the paper's position on the cause itself was clear, saying all other issues "will be overshadowed by the question of equal rights."

The Republican Party couldn't ignore the impact of this vast, silent demonstration either. The next day, after a long debate, convention delegates added women's suffrage to the party's platform.

Going beyond the Republicans' rather ambiguous call for equality, the Democrats advocated a constitutional amendment to secure women's political equality. Blair's innovative idea of a silent protest had worked, and women's right to vote became a leading issue in national politics. President Wilson won reelection and drafted a constitutional amendment that he put before the people. Despite the fact that only men could vote on it, the untiring efforts of prominent suffragettes such as Blair, and countless debates over the dinner table with reluctant husbands, resulted in victory for the suffragettes. On August 26, 1920, the Nineteenth Amendment to the Constitution passed, and women earned the right to participate in government.

SPRINGFIELD AND
THE GREAT STREETCAR STRIKE

1916

The men in the union hall raised their voices in angry unison. The Springfield Traction Company, which ran all the streetcars in the city, had gone too far. It was time to go on strike.

The streetcar workers had formed Division No. 691 of the Amalgamated Association of Street and Electric Railway Employees of America. Numbering almost a hundred men, they tried to meet with General Manager Anton Van Diense and other company representatives to get formal recognition, but each attempt came up against excuses or delays. Division No. 691 contained most of Springfield Traction's employees, so they felt they had a right to be heard. Company officials probably hoped that if they ignored the new local union, it would just go away, but the Amalgamated had a reputation for striking and causing disruptions in other towns.

Frustrated at being ignored, the union men gave the company a deadline of Friday, February 18, to sign the agreement or they would go on strike.

That deadline had come and gone. It was obvious that the company didn't want their shop unionized and had decided on confrontation rather than communication.

The strike started the next day. Almost everyone in the company walked out.

If the Springfield Traction Company thought the union would give in easily, it was sadly mistaken. The union rounded up old jitneys, horse-drawn carriages that were the predecessors to streetcars, to make their own transportation company.

In general, the people of Springfield rallied around the strikers. The town had gone through an industrial boom in the past few decades, becoming a regional shipping and manufacturing center and the fifth-largest city in the state. Working-class jobs back then involved long hours (sometimes up to sixteen hours a day), low pay, and uncomfortable and occasionally dangerous working conditions. Springfield had a large working-class population, and the city's residents saw unions as their only safety net in a land of greedy companies and little public welfare.

On Sunday Springfield mayor Thomas Bowman called a meeting of the two sides. Union officials showed up, but company officials didn't, causing the mayor to launch into an angry diatribe against Springfield Traction in the press. On Tuesday, the fourth day of the strike, more than three thousand workers from dozens of local unions marched through town to a cheering crowd of supporters.

Springfield Traction realized the union wasn't going to back down and signed the agreement the following day, after getting a section added saying any man violating company rules could be discharged or suspended. The union got their own clause added outlining an appeal system in case that happened. Exuberant at their quick victory, the strikers promptly went back to work. The harmony was not to last.

In September the company fired Stanley Jones, a secretary, claiming he had mismanaged funds and didn't wear the proper uniform. The union immediately went to Van Diense and asked for a review of the case, but he refused, citing the clause in the contract stating that any employee breaking company rules could be fired. The union complained that the contract also stipulated a review in such cases, and that the company was essentially saying it didn't recognize the union by not honoring the contract. Still the company refused, and it got a court injunction temporarily forbidding a strike.

Van Diense and his associates seemed to be following a common tactic. A company would recognize a union in order to buy time in which to organize nonunion replacement workers from outside the community, get the government to pass rulings making it harder to strike, and then goad the union into striking. The company would then bring in the replacement workers and tie up the issue in the courts, betting the union men, not having much in the bank, would be financially forced to return to work under a new agreement favorable to the company.

When the temporary injunction expired, and still without any agreement about Jones, the union went on strike on October 5.

Soon Springfield began to fill up with replacement workers hired by the company. Most had no experience running streetcars, and on the first day of the strike, only two cars were in service. The strikebreakers, contemptuously called "scabs," mostly acted as armed guards in case of trouble. As more strikebreakers came into town, the company was able to restore full service.

But the jitneys came out again, and although they were slower and less comfortable than electric trolleys, many passengers chose to show their solidarity with the union by riding them.

Days turned into weeks, and the union men started feeling the pinch. Working for the jitney service brought in some money, and sympathizers helped out with donations, but with families to feed and bills to pay, the men started to lose patience. On Halloween night there was a small, drunken riot downtown between union men and strikebreakers. Perhaps out of sympathy with the strikers or in an attempt not to make a tense situation worse, the police didn't make any arrests, but they did close the downtown bars.

Weeks stretched into months, and on Christmas evening a streetcar driving down Monroe Street was rocked by a blast of dynamite. Windows shattered all up and down the street, and a gaping hole a foot deep in the pavement showed where the charge had been laid. Luckily nobody was hurt. Police rushed to the scene, but the strikebreakers had already taken the damaged car back to the company garage.

The strikebreakers' behavior aroused the suspicion of both the police and the populace. Why would the strikebreakers take the streetcar away from the blast, essentially fleeing the scene of the crime? An investigation led to a remarkable conclusion: The strikebreakers themselves had planted the charge in an effort to discredit the union.

A witness named Millard Rowden testified that he saw a group of men led by Frank Willey, one of the strikebreakers, gathered at the blast site just before the bomb went off. The court brought these men to trial, but Rowden fled to Kansas City and couldn't be found. An angry judge charged the missing Rowden with perjury.

It is uncertain why Rowden left his hometown, but many believed he was threatened if he testified against the company men. Suspicions rose even more when a detective hired by Springfield Traction hunted Rowden down and arrested him. Rowden stood trial and was sentenced to two years in jail for perjury. The courts dropped the bombing investigation.

Exhausted by the strike and the bad publicity, the company finally came to the negotiating table. It agreed that any future conflicts would be settled by a third party; strikers who hadn't broken the law could return to work with seniority; the union would have free access to all employees; and wages would increase from 17.5 cents to 19 cents an hour, with annual raises and a bonus plan.

Triumphant, the men of the Amalgamated Association of Street and Electric Railway Employees, Division No. 691, returned to work. Jones, the fired employee, was not among them. It appears nobody in the union really cared whether he got his job back, perhaps because he really *was* incompetent. The 252-day strike was about the union, not Jones, and although it brought hardship to many, it confirmed Springfield's reputation as a union town. Shortly thereafter, streetcar workers in Kansas City and St. Louis also unionized, perhaps inspired by the struggle of Division No. 691.

LUELLA ST. CLAIR MOSS RUNS FOR CONGRESS

1922

The year 1922 was an election year like no other in Missouri. Women had recently gained the right to vote, and although they had turned out in large numbers in the 1920 election, none had run for major offices. But an ambitious and courageous woman from the middle of the state was getting ready to change that.

A Columbia schoolteacher and women's rights activist named Luella St. Clair Moss declared her candidacy for the congressional seat in the Eighth District. If she won, she would be the first woman to go to Washington to represent Boone, Camden, Cole, Cooper, Miller, Morgan, Moniteau, and Osage counties. In fact, she would be the first Missouri woman ever sent to Congress.

Her path would not be easy. Running as a Democrat, she needed to beat two other candidates in the primary. Charles Dewey was a well-connected farmer and life insurance agent from Jefferson City, and Judge E. M. Zevely had his own newspaper, the *Unterrified Democrat*, to boost his cause. Even if she won the primary and secured her party's nomination, she would still have to beat popular Republican incumbent Sid Roach, who had won by a landslide in 1920. One final obstacle weighed on her mind—were the voters ready to cast a ballot for a woman?

St. Clair Moss had some strengths to work from. She was highly respected in Boone County, the most populous county in the district, because of her presidency of Christian College (now Columbia College). During her many years as president, she had increased enrollment, bought new buildings, and doubled the size of the faculty. People also knew her for her charitable and civic service, and as a female candidate she was sure to get a lot of attention from the press.

This last asset was vital. Women were newcomers to politics, but many had already made a name for themselves as journalists, including a reporter for the *St. Louis Post-Dispatch* named Clair Kennamore, who wrote under the name Marguerite Martyn. Kennamore wrote several positive articles about St. Clair Moss that brought the candidate's views to the attention of a wide audience. St. Clair Moss herself wrote a series of articles called "Political Pointers," basically short advertisements for her campaign that were printed in almost a dozen papers.

Even Republican papers had good things to say about her. The *Moniteau County Herald* called her "a clever woman . . . capable and sincere" but couldn't help adding, "While there is much feeling against women holding office in Missouri, not much can be said in favor of the two men who will run against her in the primary."

Throughout her campaign she made her platform clear. Her main concern was a proposed tariff on foreign goods. She opposed it, she said, because American companies were strong enough to stand up to foreign competition and if that competition was taken away, they would use the opportunity to raise prices. She also would fight to lower railway shipping rates to help farmers, work with other countries to avoid war, and try to bring more women into the political process.

Her clear message and use of the media, plus a tireless round of thirty-six speeches, visits to forty-five towns, and traveling twenty-two thousand miles around the district, won the day. She polled first in every county, beating Dewey and Zevely by more than two thousand votes each. Zevely showed himself to be a good loser by using his newspaper to support her race against Roach.

St. Clair Moss knew that the fight against the Republican incumbent would be a difficult one and set off on the campaign trail right away, this time bringing along Kennamore on a tour of the rural Ozarks. Kennamore joked in one of her articles that St. Clair Moss would win because "any good housekeeper ought to be able to get rid of Roaches." The candidate spent much of her time in rural areas, assuming that her base of support in Boone County was secure and that she needed to convince the conservative rural vote that a woman could, and should, sit in Congress.

One rather disappointing stop was the Democratic State Convention in Excelsior Springs, where delegates met to agree on the party's platform. Although women were allowed to vote and even run for office, party rules forbade them from voting on party policy. The male delegates charitably allowed women to attend the convention but did not allow them to have any say in the actual decisions.

The campaign trail proved more gratifying. Wherever she went, the novelty of a female candidate drew crowds, but St. Clair Moss had to ask herself whether the attention would turn into votes on Election Day. She challenged Roach to a public debate in order to show herself the better person for the job, but Roach declined.

After an exhausting tour of the outlying counties, St. Clair Moss concentrated the last few days of her campaign on her core areas—Columbia, Ashland, and Jefferson City. Unsure of the rural voters, who liked her farm policies but could not be relied on to back her, she wanted to get as many votes as possible from the more urban, populated areas. The League of Women Voters worked day and night to rally women to vote, and the night before Election Day it appeared to be a close race.

But it was not to be. When the tallies came in, St. Clair Moss had lost by 4,368 votes, a considerable margin. Only Boone County gave a majority of votes to her, while Roach carried all seven other counties.

It's difficult to say how much St. Clair Moss's gender worked against her. Roach was a popular incumbent with an experienced and well-organized campaign, so anyone would have had a hard time beating him. It wasn't until 1952 that a woman from Missouri would represent the state in Congress. That honor fell to Leonor K. Sullivan, who served twelve terms until her retirement in 1976. The main legacy of Luella St. Clair Moss was that she opened the door, proving a woman could run a viable campaign. Even men learned from her. Her chauffeur on all those thousands of miles of backcountry canvassing was John Dalton, who went on to become governor in 1960 and attributed much of his knowledge of politics to what he had learned on the road with Missouri's first female candidate for Congress.

THE CARDINALS'
FIRST WORLD SERIES

1926

As the colors of fall faded and frost glittered on the morning grass, folks in Missouri knew it was close to World Series season. This time it was certain to be a classic: The St. Louis Cardinals faced the battle-tested New York Yankees. Families stayed home to listen to the games, and other fans crowded into bars and diners, where the usual babble of voices was stilled as every ear was turned toward the radio. Barbershops, a popular place for socializing in those days, welcomed plenty of extra business as customers hung about to listen to the latest news.

Everyone knew that the Cardinals were fighting an uphill battle. The Yankees had a batting lineup dubbed "Murderers' Row," featuring the legendary Babe Ruth, who had batted .372 that season with 47 homers and 146 RBI, and first baseman Lou Gehrig, who had batted .313 with 112 RBI, including 20 triples, the most in the American League that year.

Cardinals manager/second baseman Rogers Hornsby had some worries about his own team, too. His main pitcher was Grover

Cleveland Alexander, a thirty-nine-year-old veteran who got drunk so often the Cubs had sold him to St. Louis in the middle of the 1926 season for only $4,000. The team also had several rookies, who had never played in a championship game.

But not all the clouds were dark. Hornsby believed in Alexander, who had been the best pitcher in the league ten years before and who, when sober, could still throw with the best of them. Backing him was the solid pitching of Jess Haines. Hornsby himself was an excellent player who would have a .358 career batting average, a feat beaten only by Ty Cobb.

Opening in Yankee Stadium on October 2, the Series did not start off well for the Cardinals. The Yankees won 2–1, but the next day the Cardinals rallied for a 6–2 win. Then the action moved to St. Louis's Sportsman's Park. Game 3 proved another reassuring Cardinals win, this time 4–0, but the Yankees stomped them 10–5 in Game 4, with Babe Ruth hitting three home runs—a first in a World Series game. The Cardinals lost again to the Yankees, 3–2, in ten innings in Game 5.

The action then moved back to New York, where the Cardinals crushed the Yankees 10–2 in Game 6. Alexander, pleased with his excellent pitching that day, went out on a bender.

Now the series was tied at 3–3. Game 7, on October 10, would settle it.

During the first inning of that final game, the Cardinals managed only a single, while the Yankees did a bit better. Their first two batters were caught out, and Haines decided to walk Babe Ruth. But the next batter, Bob Meusel, hit a single to center while Ruth tore around the diamond to third. Lou Gehrig was up next, but disaster was averted when he grounded out.

The second inning saw three outs in a row, with no Cardinals making it even to first. Realizing the game wasn't going well, Haines strode out to the pitcher's mound and promptly struck out the first Yankee batter. The next batter got a single, but he was tagged out as he tried to steal second. After another single, an out brought the game to the third inning.

Now things were warming up. The Cardinals advanced players to second with only one out, but fans groaned in disappointment when the next two batters were caught out. The first two Yankees went down as well, but then Babe Ruth stepped up to the plate and batted a homer. Good fielding by the Cards brought a quick finish to the inning, but they now trailed 1–0.

The Cardinals needed to do something quick. The first batter up was Hornsby, who grounded out. Jim Bottomley hit a single, and Hi Bell reached on an error and went to first, putting Bottomley on second. Chick Hafey got a single, and now the bases were loaded.

This was the Cardinals' big chance, and they didn't let it slip away. Bob O'Farrell reached on an error, and Jim Bottomley scored, with Bell and Hafey getting to second and third. Tommy Thevenow hit a single, and both Bell and Hafey rushed to home. The score was now 3–1, but Haines struck out and Thevenow was forced, bringing the Yankees to bat.

All the Cardinals had to do now was keep their lead. Haines walked Gehrig, the Yankees' next batter flied out to center, and then another went out with a grounder that nevertheless allowed Gehrig to reach second before the Cardinals shortstop caught a line ball and brought the inning to a close.

If the Cardinals hoped to widen their lead, they were soon disappointed as the Yankees nailed down three batters in a row. The Yankees didn't do much better, with only a single, and then a walk for Ruth before they got three outs. The Cardinals were up again.

Still the Cardinals couldn't repeat their performance in the fourth inning and only managed a single. Now it was the Yankees' turn.

Gehrig grounded out, and Tony Lazzeri struck out. But with time running short, the Yankees turned up the heat. Joe Dugan singled, followed by a double by Hank Severeid that brought Dugan home, making the score 3–2. Radio listeners all across Missouri breathed a sigh of relief when Ben Paschal grounded out.

The Cardinals couldn't widen their lead, getting only a single in the top of the seventh inning, while the Yankees got a man on first, and then to second after a sacrifice bunt. Facing Ruth again, Haines did what he usually did and walked him. The famous batter was then forced, and Haines walked Gehrig.

With two outs and St. Louis still leading, things were looking good, but the Cardinals had a new problem. Haines had been seen gritting his teeth for the last several pitches, and it turned out he had worn away the skin of his forefinger. The soft flesh beneath had been rubbed raw by his fiery pitches, and the wound started to bleed. He had pitched heroically the whole game, but now his throws became erratic. With too much at stake, Hornsby brought in Alexander to replace Haines on the pitcher's mound. If Alexander was hungover from the night before, he didn't show it. He promptly struck out Lazzeri, ending the seventh inning.

The top of the eighth still saw the Cardinals ahead, but only by one run—this was the type of close game the Yankees thrived on. Hornsby singled, then got to second on a sacrifice bunt, and then, after an out to center, made it to third on a Hafey single. But Hafey got forced out, and the Yankees took their turn at bat. Another chance to widen the lead had slipped away.

Alexander's pitching kept New York from making any solid connections. Dugan grounded out, and the next two went down on popped flies.

It was now the top of the ninth. The Cardinals had one last chance to widen the lead, but Thevenow, Alexander, and Holm were all caught out in rapid succession. By this time Missourians all across the state gripped their radios in terror. It was up to the Cardinals' fielding to save the day.

First up for the Yankees was Earle Combs, who grounded out. Mark Koenig also grounded out. It was now two outs for the Yankees in the bottom of the ninth, with St. Louis leading 3–2. At this point the worst possible thing happened—Babe Ruth stepped up to the plate. Perhaps remembering Ruth's feat in Game 4, Alexander wisely decided to walk him. That must have hurt the Babe's ego, because he promptly tried to steal second. He was good at stealing, managing to pull it off about half of the time, but Cardinals catcher O'Farrell spotted him and whipped the ball to second baseman Hornsby, who caught it just as Ruth was sliding toward the plate. Hornsby tagged his foot, and it was all over. Everywhere in Missouri fans cheered around their radios. The Cardinals had won their first-ever World Series!

BREAKING
THE PENDERGAST MACHINE

1939

In the 1930s Kansas City boasted a second name, "Tom's Town," and everyone knew who Tom was—Thomas Pendergast, the head of a corrupt political machine that held the city in a vise grip. He ran the Democratic Party in the city and in Jackson County. When Pendergast wanted a man elected to office, people flocked to the polls to vote for him, sometimes more than once, and votes for opposing candidates disappeared like mist in the morning.

Once elected, these men always made sure that lucrative government contracts went to companies Pendergast and his friends owned. It had been this way for decades, ever since the machine first rose to power under the rule of Tom's big brother Jim in the 1890s. Republicans and reform-minded Democrats hated Pendergast's political dominance, but there wasn't much they could do. Opposing Pendergast could be very unhealthy.

Besides, it was easy to like Tom Pendergast. He was no ordinary crook. To his friends he was affable and loyal and could open doors for their careers. He took special care of his constituents as well, serving up more than 2,500 turkey dinners every Christmas to needy families, providing jobs to blacks and Italian immigrants who were turned away by more intolerant employers, and sponsoring social clubs for middle-class neighborhoods. More important, during the dark days of the Depression his connections in the state capital meant a large portion of federal relief and work projects ended up in Kansas City and Jackson County. So what if the building contracts used his own Ready Mixed Concrete Company? While the rest of the state languished in economic hard times, most people in Tom's area of control had money to spend. And thanks to Pendergast's liberal policies concerning saloons, jazz bars, and gambling houses, they had plenty of places in which to spend it.

Pendergast worked hard to build up his influence. He managed to get Guy Brasfield Park elected governor, and this favor brought in those hefty federal relief contracts as well as influence across the state. But Tom Pendergast wasn't the only power broker in Missouri. He might have ruled the roost in "Tom's Town," but other forces, both Republican and Democrat, wanted to see him fall.

Besides tackling the Depression, newly elected President Franklin Delano Roosevelt wanted to stop a wave of high-profile crimes perpetrated by famous gangsters. Under the direction of J. Edgar Hoover and attorney general Homer Cummings, the Bureau of Investigation (the precursor to the FBI) hunted down a whole slew of violent bank robbers. They went after political machines, too, in response to widespread complaints over election fraud. Kansas City became an obvious target because of Pendergast's notoriety and the fact that it had the highest murder rate in the country. The Bureau soon found gambling houses, slot machines, and illegal saloons operating all over the city and suspected that a single organization ran them all.

The federal government had a local ally in Maurice Milligan, whom FDR had appointed district attorney for the Western District of Missouri. His brother Jacob was running in the Democratic primary for Senate against Pendergast's chosen candidate, a young judge named Harry Truman. The Milligans were friends with Senator Bennett Clark, who wanted to wrest control of Missouri's federal patronage from the Kansas City machine.

Both candidates accused each other of being puppets for corrupt men. Truman tried to distance himself from the Kansas City machine (something that would plague him even after he became president) by talking about his support for Roosevelt's New Deal policies and how they were lifting the nation out of the Depression. But the fact that Truman got 137,000 votes in Jackson County—while Milligan and another candidate, Cochran, got only 11,000 votes between them—indicated that something was up. Truman won the primary statewide, too, but by a much closer margin, and went on to win the general election.

The Kansas City municipal election was even more one-sided, with accusations of vote fraud and that the machine had hired thugs to intimidate voters (in fact, two people were killed and eleven were sent to the hospital).

Roosevelt's federal work programs made him very popular in Missouri, and with Pendergast. When Roosevelt was reelected in 1936, investigative reporters for the *Kansas City Star* claimed fifty thousand votes were false. They even found thirty registered voters who shared the same address—a funeral home.

Maurice Milligan took a close look at the numbers. Although it appeared that Roosevelt really did win, he discovered many irregularities. Some districts showed only a couple of votes for a Republican candidate while his Democratic opponent got hundreds. In many districts Republicans running for different offices all got the exact same number of votes. Milligan brought the matter to court.

The first trial was of John Drummond, a Democratic precinct captain, and Edson Walker, a Democratic judge. Chloe Albright, a

Republican judge who worked with them tallying the votes, testified that Walker arrogantly told him they weren't going to count any ballots; Walker then made up some numbers and threatened Albright with a "one-way ride" if he didn't sign the official form verifying the count. Both Walker and Drummond got two years in prison.

More convictions followed—259 of them, in fact. Although none of the defendants pointed a finger at Pendergast, he could feel the noose tightening.

Governor Lloyd Stark, originally a Pendergast man, saw which way the wind was blowing and appointed an election board to oversee Kansas City. During the 1938 primaries the Democrats became bitterly divided between Pendergast's supporters and those who saw his machine as an embarrassment and an obstacle to their own advancement. Stark's election board threw out thousands of votes, and Democratic organizations and voters outside of Jackson County turned against the Pendergast machine.

With his machine seriously weakened, the public turning against him, and his health deteriorating, Pendergast now found himself the target of a Treasury Department investigation. As it turned out, he had accepted more than $500,000 in cash from allies and a crooked insurance scam. Pendergast had lost too much influence to fight a powerful federal department, and in 1939 a court sentenced him to fifteen months in prison, a rather modest fine of $10,000, and five years' probation. Like the notorious gangster Al Capone of Chicago, he didn't get caught for racketeering, assault, or any other serious crime, but for lying on his tax forms. He died in 1945, his power broken.

FROM MISSOURI TO
THE WHITE HOUSE

1948

President Harry Truman faced some serious problems. The Missouri native was running for reelection against a popular Republican opponent, his own Democratic Party had split between him and two other candidates, his ratings in the polls remained low as usual, and a worsening situation overseas threatened to end in disaster, if not World War III.

Even his own family didn't think he could win reelection, but at least they had the courtesy to keep their opinions to themselves.

Nobody else did. All the political analysts, academics, and polling companies predicted he would lose, and few newspapers endorsed him. Even Missouri newspapers turned away from the man born in Lamar and raised in Independence.

Truman's troubles had begun shortly after he assumed the presidency. In 1944, at the height of World War II, he had been elected as Franklin Delano Roosevelt's vice president. The popular wartime president died the following year, and Truman took over the Oval

Office. So, in fact, he had never been elected to the presidency. His popularity remained fairly high as he oversaw the end of the war, but people questioned his policies after that. Many conservatives didn't like his outspoken support for civil rights, and liberals didn't like his opposition to the Soviet Union, a nation that many saw as a valuable ally in the war against Hitler but that Truman saw as a dangerous threat to world security.

These divisions led to a schism in the Democratic Party. Henry Wallace, leading the progressive wing of the party, split off first, criticizing Truman's "containment" policy against the Soviets as dangerous and intolerant. Strom Thurmond broke away next, leading his so-called "Dixiecrats," Southern conservatives who objected to Truman's support of desegregation and civil rights.

In the face of a divided Democratic Party, the Republicans looked sure to win. They had already taken control of the House and Senate in the midterm elections, and everyone predicted that voters were tired of sixteen years of Democratic presidencies and were eager for a change. The Republican presidential candidate was New York governor Thomas Dewey, who had gained national attention for his long crusade against gangsters and corrupt politicians. He had even given the highly popular Roosevelt a run for his money in the 1944 presidential election.

Despite all of these problems, Truman had no intention of giving up. He fought a hard campaign in the primaries and managed to get the party's nomination, although the debate over whether to nominate him took so long that Truman didn't get to make his acceptance speech until after 2:00 a.m. To celebrate his nomination, his supporters released fifty "doves of peace" from under a Liberty Bell made of flowers. As they flew over the crowd, they bombarded the delegates, leaving disgusting splotches on their hair and fine suits. One "dove of peace," in a fit of bad symbolism, dropped dead.

But Truman wasn't a superstitious man, and he never knew when to quit. Wallace and Thurmond stayed in the race, Dewey led in the polls, and even Roosevelt's widow, the much-respected Eleanor, refused to endorse him—but Truman simply saw all of this as a challenge.

The Republicans' big weakness, he knew, was Congress. They had been in charge of both the Senate and the House for two years and had managed to alienate blacks, laborers, farmers, the poor, and a great many other groups. Truman decided to equate Dewey with the Republican Congress and raised the specter of what government would be like if the Republicans controlled everything. He started right in with his acceptance speech, saying the party "helps the rich and sticks a knife in the back of the poor."

Truman also criticized Congress for blocking many of his popular ideas.

> *The Republican platform comes out for slum clearance and low-rental housing. I have been trying to get them to pass this housing bill ever since they met the first time, and it is still resting in the rules committee. . . . The Republican platform urges expanding and increasing Social Security benefits . . . and yet when they had the opportunity they took seven hundred and fifty thousand people off the Social Security rolls.*

He spent a great deal of his campaign in farming states, including his home state of Missouri, criticizing Congress for not passing bills to help farmers and implying that Dewey would do the same. Congress had reduced the federal grain-storage capacity by more than 80 percent, and when farmers had a bumper crop that year, they couldn't store their grain and had to sell it at below-market prices.

In Iowa Truman remarked that they had "stuck a pitchfork in the farmers' backs." His pro-farm stance also brought him support in Southern states that might have voted for Thurmond.

Truman also stood up to Congress on several occasions. When he vetoed the Taft-Hartley Labor Act, an act designed to reduce the power of unions, he brought organized labor onto his side, especially after Congress overrode his veto. In May he recognized the new state of Israel, and in July he ended segregation in the armed forces and federal government, gaining him the Jewish and black vote. He even called a special session of Congress to give lawmakers a chance to pass various popular acts, such as raising the minimum wage from 40 to 75 cents an hour and allocating $300 million in education funds to the states. He knew they wouldn't, and when his prediction came true, he called them the "do-nothing Congress."

Truman got some unexpected help from the Soviet Union. In February the Soviets backed a coup in Czechoslovakia, expanding their influence into central Europe, and in June they stopped surface traffic into West Berlin. The city, occupied by Allied troops since the end of World War II, was divided into East Berlin, controlled by the Soviets, and West Berlin, controlled by the United States, Britain, and France, but surrounded by Soviet-controlled countryside. The Soviets wanted West Berlin and by cutting it off from the outside world hoped to starve it into submission. Truman wasn't about to let that happen, and started the famous Berlin Airlift to fly supplies into the city. While this brought the United States into conflict with the Soviet Union, the Soviets eventually backed down. Truman's stubbornness against Soviet aggression gained him the support of German-Americans, who traditionally voted Republican, and made Wallace's friendly policies toward the Soviets look foolish.

Truman's ratings in the polls rose after the United States launched the Berlin Airlift. People began to see him as a strong leader who would keep the country safe in uncertain times.

Truman and his team campaigned hard, crisscrossing the state by train to meet voters. Dewey, on the other hand, convinced he was going to win, ran a lackluster campaign and rarely took a firm stance so that he wouldn't be trapped by anything he said once he became president.

Truman ended his campaign with a speech at Kiel Auditorium in St. Louis. He declared, "I can't tell you how very much I appreciate this reception on my return to my home state. . . . I know when Missouri feels this way, we are on the road to victory."

He probably didn't feel as confident as he sounded. On election night the numbers were the closest they had been in more than three decades, and the president went to bed not knowing if he would spend the next four years sleeping in the White House or back in Independence.

He woke up the next morning to find the *Chicago Tribune* had printed a banner headline stating "Dewey Defeats Truman." Other papers posted similar reports.

But they, and all the political analysts and academics, had gotten it wrong. While Dewey carried many of the industrial states in the Northeast, and Thurmond won four Southern states, Truman swept the farm states and the West. Ninety percent of blacks had voted for him, and large numbers of undecided voters had thrown their support behind him at the last minute. A triumphant president gleefully held up a copy of the *Chicago Tribune* to photographers and joked, "This is one for the books."

JESSE JAMES IS ALIVE!

1949

September 5, 1949, was a big day at Meramec Caverns in Stanton, Missouri. An eager crowd was on hand to see famous outlaw Jesse James and wish him a happy 102nd birthday.

But wait! Doesn't every Missourian know that Jesse James was shot from behind by Robert Ford on April 3, 1882?

Not true, said the aged "Jesse" as he lay in his bed surrounded by old guns, saddles, and photographs. Another man had been killed in his place. As the crowd stood entranced, James told the incredible tale of how he had eluded justice all those years, traveled the world, and served as a fighter pilot during World War I while in his sixties. Two other members of his gang were there, too: Cole Younger (aged 106) and John Trammell (aged 110).

None of these men were who they said they were, and they were all decades younger than the ripe old ages they claimed. The whole thing had been thought up as a marketing stunt for Meramec Caverns.

This wasn't the first time someone had claimed to be Jesse James. There had been several imposters over the years. The man in

Meramec Caverns seems to have taken his story from an earlier James imposter named John James, who used Jesse's persona while he did rope tricks on stage in the 1920s. He even performed a bit of real outlawry. In 1926, when he was seventy-nine, John James borrowed fifty cents from a young man named Charles Shelton. When Shelton demanded his money back and threatened James, the old man pulled out a gun and killed him. The judge only gave John James a year in prison, probably because of the threatening nature of the incident, and after James served his year, he was paroled. He soon stopped seeing his parole officer and left town.

John James later reappeared, boasting he was really the famous outlaw. He claimed that another outlaw named Charles Bigelow, who looked like Jesse, had been killed in his place so that he could live a peaceful life safe from the law. Jesse allowed his friend Robert Ford to take credit for "killing" him so he could get the reward money, while Jesse's family and neighbors all participated in the hoax.

As incredible as this story sounds, some people believed it. John James was quite successful for a time on the lecture and sideshow circuit until one fateful day in Excelsior Springs, Missouri. John James was giving his spiel when a woman in the audience stood up and challenged him. It was Annie James, wife of Jesse's brother Frank, and she presented the imposter with one of Jesse's boots. The real outlaw had unusually small feet and wore a size seven and half boot. Annie challenged John James to put it on. Of course, it didn't fit, and he was laughed off stage.

You would think that would have been the end of the story, but John James continued his tour, hooking up for a time with "The Flying Preacher" Robert Highley. He then foolishly returned to Excelsior Springs in 1933 and asked to spend a night in the local jail as a publicity stunt.

He should have stayed away. Robert James, son of Frank James, paid him a visit. Robert grilled him about his past, and John James made several basic mistakes. He didn't even know the middle name of Jesse's half-brother Archie Peyton Samuel, who had been killed by a Pinkerton bomb at the James home. Undaunted, John James kept up his facade. He was becoming increasingly erratic, however, and ended his days at Arkansas State Mental Hospital, where he died in 1947.

The very next year, the man who would celebrate a dead man's birthday in Meramec Caverns came forth and claimed he was the real Jesse James. His actual name was J. Frank Dalton. Little is known about him. Some people who saw him on his speaking tour said they recognized him as a carnival barker from Texas, but even these stories are poorly documented. It appears Dalton posed as Billy the Kid for a time, even though that outlaw had been shot dead in 1881. Promoter Orvus Lee Howk convinced him to change his story and pretend he was the more famous and better-loved Jesse James. Furthermore, Howk claimed he was Dalton's grandson and took on the name Jesse James III.

Dalton was knowledgeable about the Wild West and had obviously studied the Jesse James story. He had even written a couple of pamphlets about the famous Missouri outlaw, including details about his death at the hands of Robert Ford. Those early writings got swept under the rug as Dalton recycled John James's story of Charles Bigelow getting killed in Jesse's place.

The tour started in Oklahoma and became a national media sensation. The reporters who flocked to interview Dalton probably weren't fooled, but they knew what sold papers. So did Howk. He took the old man on a nationwide tour, making numerous live appearances, including one at the Tennessee State Fair, and even landing interviews on nationally syndicated radio shows.

Like John James before him, Dalton got tripped up by someone more knowledgeable. Wild West researcher and James biographer

Homer Croy grilled him and came away convinced that Dalton was a fraud.

Besides some gaps in his knowledge, there was also the problem that Jesse James was known to have been missing the tip of his left middle finger, the result of an accident while cleaning a gun. Luckily the index finger of Dalton's left hand was mutilated so he simply claimed that all the contemporary accounts and biographers had their facts wrong about which finger was damaged. He also explained away the lack of any bullet wounds (Jesse took several slugs in his time) by claiming that he had had skin grafts to remove them. Undaunted, Dalton headed to Missouri to do his show at Meramec Caverns.

It was a big hit. Dalton even applied to a Missouri court to have his name changed back to Jesse James. The judge ruled that if he really was Jesse James, there was no need for a legal name change, and if he wasn't Jesse James, then he was trying to perpetrate a fraud on the court. That ended that idea.

Dalton died in Texas in 1951, still claiming he was the real Jesse James. The epitaph on his grave in Granbury, Texas, reads "Jesse Woodson James, Sept. 5, 1847–Aug. 15, 1951, supposedly killed in 1882."

Meramec Caverns manager and promoter Rudy Turilli kept the legend alive with a book titled *The Truth about Jesse James,* in which he made the bold statement that he would pay $10,000 to anyone who could prove Dalton wasn't Jesse James. Members of the real James family brought Turilli to court in 1970 and won. Turilli didn't pay the reward and died two years later.

Every now and then the Jesse James conspiracy theory gets new life in some poorly researched pamphlet or magazine story. The seeds were sown for this confusion back when the real Jesse was still alive. His death was reported several times in the newspapers, only for him to reappear and rob again. The story was further muddled when other imposters pretended to be Frank James and added their own wild tales.

This is a common phenomenon. The Grand Duchess Anastasia, Adolf Hitler, Michael Jackson, and many others supposedly survived their deaths. For a time Missouri even had an Elvis is Alive Cafe & Museum. It seems the public can't let go of celebrities.

While the tales these old-timers spun are entertaining, Jesse James really was killed by Robert Ford on that fateful day in St. Joseph. Hundreds of friends, relatives, and acquaintances saw him lying in his open casket before the funeral and none said it was another man. In 1995, DNA evidence on Jesse's bones showed that he was, indeed, the man he was said to be. Except for a few willful believers, the controversy has been put to rest, and Jesse James has been laid in his grave.

BUILDING THE ARCH

1965

St. Louis was preparing for a big day as the Gateway Arch, part of the Jefferson National Expansion Memorial, would be finished in a grand ceremony. The site for the memorial had been selected in 1935 and forty blocks of old, decrepit buildings cleared away, but World War II delayed the project until 1947, when the Jefferson National Expansion Memorial Association started a competition for designs for the monument. Hundreds of architects sent in proposals, but the committee unanimously chose an arch designed by a Finnish-American named Eero Saarinen.

The arch was an innovative design that required a complex technique to build. It was to be a 630-foot tall inverted catenary curve, the shape a hanging chain takes if held at both ends. Saarinen's design called for 142 triangular sections of stainless steel, with sides 54 feet long at the base, and tapering to only 17 feet long on each side at the top. This would create a solid base and a lighter top, with the weight distributed down each leg. His blueprints called for the outer skin to be only a quarter-inch-thick stainless steel, and the inner skin of carbon steel only three-eights of an inch, a perfect thickness to ensure both lightness and strength. For the first 300 feet above ground level, the space between the two skins was filled with concrete to add stability, and above this the two layers were held together by steel joints. The foundations were set 60 feet deep to hold the Arch's 5,199 tons of steel.

A key aspect of the design is its flexibility. Strong winds are dangerous for tall structures, so they need to give a little. While this may sound frightening to anyone standing on top, if the wind is blowing at 20 mph, a not uncommon occurrence, the Arch will sway a full inch, but it can sway up to 18 inches in hurricane-force winds of 150 mph. This flexibility, and the strong foundations, mean it can also withstand an earthquake if the New Madrid fault line decides to act up again.

As Saarinen told the *St. Louis Post-Dispatch* in a January 19, 1958, interview, he wanted to "achieve the simplicity of the Washington Monument or the great pyramids of Egypt, because the simplest and purest forms last the longest, and I have always felt this arch of stainless steel would last a thousand years."

Building such an arch, in which the two bent legs would have to stand on their own until the final section was put in, was a serious engineering task, requiring a strong steel truss between the legs. Special creeper derricks equipped with cranes rode tracks up the legs to fit new pieces on the top. The vital final step of attaching the keystone section would only work, of course, if the legs were the same height.

But there was a major problem—the two legs weren't going to meet up.

The city had watched the steady climb of the two shining steel legs as they curved toward one another, and eagerly anticipated when the two eight-foot keystone sections would be put into place and the arch finally stood complete.

Tiny differences in the strength of the two legs and the effect of sunlight on the metal warped them ever so slightly, but enough to make one leg up to ten inches higher than the other.

The building committee had to think fast. The completion ceremony was due to start at 10 a.m. the next day. They met in an emergency 2 a.m. conference to decide what to do.

The committee struck upon an idea. Their problem was the heat of the sun striking the shiny metal, and who was most experienced at dealing with unwanted heat in high buildings?

Enter the St. Louis Fire Department. At 8:30 that morning they started spraying the south leg, where the sunlight was strongest, their hoses reaching up to 530 feet above the watching crowds. Every few minutes the engineers checked the south leg's level in relation to the north, until after nearly an hour they declared the legs to be equal height. The creeper derrick slowly brought the final sections up the tracks toward the last gap in the arch. As it made the half-hour trip the engineers kept a close eye on the relative levels of the legs, but the trick with the water worked, and the firefighters joined the ranks of the thousands of Missourians who could take credit for working on the nation's most unique monument.

The crane dangled the final section above the gap and slowly eased it down into place. As thousands of onlookers cheered in the park below, a troop of Boy Scouts raised an American flag over the keystone section.

The job was complete. Workers dismantled the truss, then moved the derricks down the arch, removing the track as they went. In only a few days, the Arch stood alone, shining in the Missouri sun.

MISSOURI: THE FLOOD STATE

1993

The town of Hannibal felt as though it was on the receiving end of a bad April Fool's joke. On the first of the month the Mississippi rose to sixteen feet, the official marking point for a flood. But this was no joke; everyone could see it for themselves on the markers that stood on the banks of the river. Heavy rains in the north mixed with melting spring snow, worsened by increased runoff from deforestation. All of these factors contributed to the flood, and none of them showed any signs of letting up.

Less than a week later the river stood at 18.8 feet and rising. Minor flooding occurred along both the Mississippi and Missouri Rivers. The townspeople of Hannibal, however, hoped they would be spared having the Big Muddy in their living rooms. The town had recently built a giant twelve-foot-high flood wall that could close its gates and seal off the town if the river rose much higher.

It did, but the townspeople were dismayed to find that their wall had a weak spot. Bear Creek, a tributary of the Mississippi, ran through part of town on its way to the great river. It would have cost too much to build a flood wall along its length, so when Mississippi River water backed up into the creek on April 13, the waters flowed unimpeded out of the creek's banks. It wasn't damaging any houses yet, but if it rose much higher, it would. Ominously, the next day a thunderstorm added an inch of rainfall to the already swollen creek.

With the National Weather Service predicting more rain, on April 16 the town brought out some cranes to lower the floodgates, giant slabs of concrete that filled the gaps in the wall. Although these would protect the part of town not near Bear Creek, they also cut off the homes and businesses that had foolishly been built on the floodplain. In the past decade more than two hundred of these structures had been moved to higher ground, but some remained. No amount of engineering would be able to save those. Continuing rain swelled the Mississippi to more than twenty-two feet, and on April 22 all the homes on South Main Street, near Bear Creek, had to be evacuated.

Then, at the beginning of May, the river level began to drop, enough that on May 21 the town removed the floodgates. It seemed as though the worst had come and gone. Except for some minor flooding and a great deal of inconvenience, the hardy river town appeared to have weathered another of its periodic floods.

But it was not to be. On June 18 a fierce storm dumped more than two inches of rain onto Hannibal in as many hours, filling basements and making streets impassable. Weather forecasters predicted more rain, and the floodgates went back in. By the end of the month, Bear Creek had risen enough to claim some of the homes near its banks.

Across the region the same thing was happening. Unprepared towns were hit hard, and some people drowned when they tried to drive through flooded streets. River traffic stopped as boat captains couldn't guarantee their cargo's safety on America's busiest waterway. The river had become unpredictable, with new currents and eddies as well as hidden dangers such as floating trees and other debris.

The Army Corps of Engineers shook their heads in despair. This was the Mississippi of old—dangerous, unpredictable, unforgiving—but a hundred years of clearance and channeling by the corps and other government agencies should have fixed all that. Levees were bursting all along the Mississippi and Missouri Rivers, destroying crops, homes, and parkland. But the worst was not yet over as the waters continued to rise.

Officials evacuated the nearby town of LaGrange as volunteers and the National Guard started sandbagging along Route 168. The Mark Twain Memorial Bridge, the town's main connection with Illinois, had to be closed because even it was flooded. Most of the events in the town's annual Tom Sawyer Days had to be called off. Fearing the floods, tourists chose to go somewhere a bit drier.

Hannibal's most famous resident, Mark Twain, had been a steamboat captain and had warned of how dangerous the river could be and that those living near it must respect its power. Now Hannibal's modern-day boat captains were forced to learn this. On July 9 the raging river snapped the moorings of the town's marina, carrying the boats along only to smash them against the shore miles downstream. The next day, with levees breaking all up and down the two rivers and whole towns going underwater, President Bill Clinton declared the region a disaster area, making it eligible for federal aid.

Although Missourians welcomed the help, they were already helping themselves. Volunteer crews built walls of sandbags along highways and around vulnerable buildings. It was a grueling task. Once filled with sand, each bag weighed up to thirty pounds and had to be hauled into place. Then the process was repeated thousands of times for up to twelve hours a day. Other volunteers helped residents move their possessions away from threatened homes or worked in food kitchens or emergency shelters.

July 16 would be the high point, when the river rose to 31.3 feet and broke through the levee at nearby West Quincy, flooding fourteen thousand acres and cutting off the last remaining bridge to Illinois within a hundred miles.

Hannibal's flood protection still kept most of the town dry as the water rose to an all-time high of 31.8 feet on July 25, but a nearby levee at Sny suddenly gave way, and the river rushed in to inundate more than forty-five thousand acres. Caught unawares, people had to flee at a moment's notice.

Four of the levee workers weren't quick enough and had to climb a tree or perch atop a nearby tractor as the waters shot past. Luckily for them, a helicopter spotted them and plucked them up in a dramatic rescue.

While it didn't seem so at the time, the worst was over. After July 16 the water gradually receded, and by September 23 the river had dropped below flood levels to 15.7 feet. But that same day a storm dropped two inches of rain on Hannibal, as if Mother Nature wanted to remind the townspeople who calls the shots.

All that was left to do was to clean up. Most of Hannibal survived, but homes near Bear Creek or along the floodplain were destroyed. Many surviving houses had to be abandoned. Everything was caked in mud. Peeling wallpaper turned fuzzy with mold, and nothing could salvage the soaked carpeting and furniture. The buildings that were strong enough to survive with their foundations and walls intact had to be thoroughly cleaned and disinfected before they were safe for human habitation.

Across ten states every town had a similar story, or a worse one. The Mississippi and Missouri Rivers flooded an estimated eight million acres, forcing seventy thousand people to evacuate and killing forty-eight. More than thirty thousand Missourians lost their jobs because their place of work was destroyed. On one grisly day the water washed away hundreds of caskets from a historic cemetery in Hardin, sending them floating downriver. More than two hundred were never recovered. For Hannibal it could have been much worse, but the townspeople's foresight in building a flood wall and moving buildings off the floodplain had saved them, at least that time.

MISSOURI FACTS AND TRIVIA

- In 1821 Missouri became the twenty-fourth state to join the United States.

- Missouri is nicknamed the "Show-Me State." Local lore states that Congressman Willard Vandiver (served 1896–1902) started the expression when he said in a speech, "I am from Missouri. You have got to show me." Actually, it was already a common expression in Missouri at the time.

- The state motto is *Salus Populi Suprema Lex Esto* ("The Welfare of the People Shall Be the Supreme Law").

- The state mineral is galena, which is mined for its high lead content. Southeast Missouri has the largest galena reserves in the world.

- President Harry Truman originally thought of becoming a professional musician. Although he ended up in a rather different career, he was an accomplished piano player with a wide repertoire. However, he often pretended that he didn't know how to play the "Missouri Waltz," the state song, because he thought it was "terrible music."

- The state musical instrument is the fiddle, which was often the only instrument in frontier towns and is still a favorite instrument in the Ozarks today.

- In the early pioneering days, money was so scarce that many people paid their bills with postage stamps.

- The First Bank of Missouri issued a $3 bill in 1817.

- There's a long-standing Ozark tradition that if you want to get baptized in winter, you don't let a bit of ice in the river stop you. Just cut a hole and get dipped!

- The first case heard at the Boone County courthouse was against a man who tried to defraud the government. There was a bounty on wolves, and he brought in a wolf pelt he had cut in two, claiming he had killed two little wolves when in fact he had shot only one big wolf.

- Back in the early nineteenth century, people used to go to a sandbar on the Mississippi River called "Bloody Island" to fight duels. Spectators often stood atop Big Mound, a prehistoric burial mound in St. Louis that offered a good view of the island.

- The Canton Ferry, established 1844, is the longest continuously operating ferry service on the Mississippi. It used to be operated by two horses on treadmills that turned a paddle wheel.

- The town of Brunswick celebrates its local produce with the "World's Largest Pecan," actually made of twelve thousand pounds of cement. It is twelve feet long and seven feet in diameter.

- In Sumner the "World's Largest Goose," also fake, weighs 5,500 pounds and has a sixty-five-foot wingspan. It honors the Swan Lake Wildlife Refuge, a favorite stopping point for Canada geese and other migratory birds.

- The engineering students at the local university in Rolla built a half-size, partial replica of Stonehenge that can calculate the correct time to within fifteen seconds.

- The Cathedral of the Prince of Peace in Highlandville is the world's smallest cathedral. Able to hold only about a dozen worshippers, this arm of the Christ Catholic Church boasts that it is "big enough to hold people of every faith."

- Branson resident Rose O'Neill developed the Kewpie doll from a character she drew for various magazines.

- Missouri is also known as the "Cave State" because of its more than five thousand caverns, the biggest being Crevice Cave in Perry County, with twenty-eight miles of tunnels and rooms. Missourians have used caves for outlaw hideouts, gunpowder mills, mushroom farms, distilleries for moonshine, and dance halls.

- Harry Truman may not have been the first Missourian to be president. When President James Polk's term expired on March 4, 1849, a Sunday, his successor, the religious Zachary Taylor, refused to be sworn in because it would count as working on the Sabbath. By law the presiding officer of the Senate, who at that time was Missourian David Rice Atchison, became president for a day. Historians debate about whether he was legally president, but by all accounts he didn't do much during his one day in power.

- Some of the earliest "paved" roads in Missouri were made of wooden planks. First built in 1851, these roads warped because of the weather and proved to be almost useless. Even during the short time before the roads got bent out of shape, the ride was bumpier than going over normal ground.

- The Bonne Terre Mine, an abandoned lead mine and National Historic Site, is now the largest underground lake in the world. It covers eighty square miles in five levels.

- In 1855 (some say 1856), Kansas tried to buy Kansas City from Missouri, but the state government said it wasn't for sale.

- The world's first airmail was sent by balloon from St. Louis to New York on July 1, 1859. The group of aviators lost altitude and had to throw off their ballast, which included the mail, but it was recovered later. They crashed into the treetops near Henderson, New York, but were unhurt.

- The Missouri mule, the official state animal, is descended from Mexican mules brought in on the Santa Fe Trail and bred for intelligence, endurance, and strength. They are sterile offspring of a mare and a male donkey. The offspring of a stallion and a female donkey are called hinnies.

- The famous military newspaper the *Stars and Stripes* was founded in Bloomfield, Missouri, in 1861.

- Missouri provided more soldiers for the Civil War, in proportion to its population, than any other state in either the Union or the Confederacy. Almost two hundred thousand men served, and about twenty-seven thousand died.

- In the early days of the Civil War in 1861, General John Frémont, Union commander of the Department of the West, which included Missouri, declared that slaves owned by rebels were legally free. President Lincoln made him rescind the order, and it wasn't until January 1863, sixteen months later, that the president himself freed the slaves with the Emancipation Proclamation.

- The Emancipation Proclamation signed by Lincoln freed only the slaves in the rebellious states. Missouri was not considered a rebellious state, and the buying and selling of slaves continued throughout the war. Not until after the war ended in 1865 were all slaves freed throughout the country.

- The American Legion held its first meeting on May 9, 1919, in St. Louis.

- Many of the first ragtime, blues, and jazz musicians came from Missouri, making it the leader in developing three types of music.

- Missouri Day, a special day to celebrate Missouri's history, culture, and people, is on the third Wednesday in October. But before you mark your calendars, double-check the date. When the day was first proposed by Anna Brosius Korn of Trenton, she suggested October 1. The state approved it in 1915 but decided to change it to the first Monday in October. In 1969 the date changed to the third Wednesday in October and has remained so until at least 2012.

BIBLIOGRAPHY

Mound City, the City Before St. Louis—1200

Cahokia Mounds State Historic Site, personal visit and observations by the author.

Chapman, Carl, and Eleanor Chapman. *Indians and Archaeology of Missouri.* Columbia: University of Missouri Press, 1983.

Marshall, John B. "The St. Louis Mound Group: Historical Accounts and Pictorial Descriptions." *Missouri Archaeologist* 53 (December 1992).

O'Brien, Michael, and W. Raymond Wood. *The Prehistory of Missouri.* Columbia: University of Missouri Press, 1998.

Peale, T. R. "Ancient Mounds at St. Louis, Missouri, in 1819." *Annual Report for the Smithsonian Institution for the Year, 1861.* Washington, DC: Government Printing Office, 1862.

Williams, Stephen, and John Goggin. "The Long Nosed God Mask in Eastern United States." *Missouri Archaeologist* 18, no. 3 (1956).

The Teenager Who Built a City—1764

Chouteau, Auguste. *Fragment of Col. Auguste Chouteau's Narrative of the Settlement of St. Louis: A Literal Translation from the Original French Ms., in Possession of the St. Louis Mercantile Library Association.* St. Louis: George Knapp & Co., 1858.

Christensen, Lawrence, et al. *Dictionary of Missouri Biography.* Columbia: University of Missouri Press, 1999.

Foley, William. *The Genesis of Missouri: From Wilderness Outpost to Statehood.* Columbia: University of Missouri Press, 1989.

———. *A History of Missouri. Volume I: 1673 to 1820.* Columbia: University of Missouri Press, 1971.

Foley, William, and C. David Rice. *The First Chouteaus: River Barons of Early St. Louis.* Chicago: University of Illinois Press, 1983.

Hodes, Frederick A. *Beyond the Frontier: A History of St. Louis to 1821.* Tucson: Patrice Press, 2004.

Peterson, Charles. *Colonial St. Louis: Building a Creole Capital.* 2nd ed. Tucson: Patrice Press, 1993.

The Battle of Fort San Carlos—1780

Christensen, Lawrence, et al. *Dictionary of Missouri Biography.* Columbia: University of Missouri Press, 1999.

Foley, William. *The Genesis of Missouri: From Wilderness Outpost to Statehood.* Columbia: University of Missouri Press, 1989.

———. *A History of Missouri. Volume I: 1673 to 1820.* Columbia: University of Missouri Press, 1971.

Hodes, Frederick A. *Beyond the Frontier: A History of St. Louis to 1821.* Tucson: Patrice Press, 2004.

Parkin, Robert. *The Revolution in the Environs of St. Louis.* St. Louis: St. Louis Genealogical Society, 1993.

Lewis and Clark Brave the Missouri River—1804

Denny, James. "Running the Lower Missouri River Gauntlet: The First Trial of the Lewis and Clark Expedition." *Missouri Historical Review* 98, no. 4 (July 2004).

Foley, William, "Friends and Partners: William Clark, Meriwether Lewis, and Mid-America's French Creoles." *Missouri Historical Review* 98, no. 4 (July 2004).

———. *A History of Missouri. Volume I: 1673 to 1820.* Columbia: University of Missouri Press, 1971.

Jackson, Donald, ed. *Letters of the Lewis and Clark Expedition with Related Documents, 1783–1854.* 2nd ed. Urbana: University of Illinois Press, 1978.

Moulton, Gary, ed. *The Journals of the Lewis and Clark Expedition.* Lincoln: University of Nebraska Press, 1983–1999.

Ronda, James. "St. Louis Welcomes and Toasts the Lewis and Clark Expedition: A Newly Discovered 1806 Newspaper Account." *We Proceeded On* 13 (February 1987).

Daniel Boone's Missouri Misadventure—1805

Botkin, B. A. *A Treasury of American Folklore: Stories, Ballads, and Traditions of the People.* New York: Crown Publishers, 1944.

Christensen, Lawrence, et al. *Dictionary of Missouri Biography.* Columbia: University of Missouri Press, 1999.

Faragher, John Mack. *Daniel Boone: The Life and Legend of an American Pioneer.* New York: Henry Holt, 1992.

Hammon, Neal, ed. *My Father, Daniel Boone: The Draper Interviews with Nathan Boone.* Introduction by Nelson L. Dawson. Lexington: University Press of Kentucky, 1999.

Founding Fort Osage—1808

Foley, William. *The Genesis of Missouri: From Wilderness Outpost to Statehood.* Columbia: University of Missouri Press, 1989.

———. *A History of Missouri. Volume I: 1673 to 1820.* Columbia: University of Missouri Press, 1971.

Fort Osage National Historic Landmark, personal visit and observations by the author.

Parrish, William, Charles Jones Jr., and Lawrence Christensen. *Missouri: The Heart of the Nation.* 3rd ed. Wheeling, Ill.: Harlan Davidson, 2004.

The New Madrid Earthquake—1811

Foley, William. *The Genesis of Missouri: From Wilderness Outpost to Statehood.* Columbia: University of Missouri Press, 1989.

———. *A History of Missouri. Volume I: 1673 to 1820.* Columbia: University of Missouri Press, 1971.

Parrish, William, Charles Jones Jr., and Lawrence Christensen. *Missouri: The Heart of the Nation.* 3rd ed. Wheeling, Ill.: Harlan Davidson, 2004.

Sampson, Francis. "The New Madrid and Other Earthquakes in Missouri." *Missouri Historical Review* 92, no. 3 (April 1998).

A State in the Making—1818–1821

Foley, William. *The Genesis of Missouri: From Wilderness Outpost to Statehood.* Columbia: University of Missouri Press, 1989.

———. *A History of Missouri. Volume I: 1673 to 1820.* Columbia: University of Missouri Press, 1971.

March, David, "The Admission of Missouri." *Missouri Historical Review* 65, no. 4 (July 1971).

McCandless, Perry. *A History of Missouri. Volume II: 1820 to 1860.* Columbia: University of Missouri Press, 1972.

Merkel, Benjamin. "The Abolition Aspects of Missouri's Antislavery Controversy, 1819–1865." *Missouri Historical Review* 44, no. 3 (April 1950).

Missouri Gazette & Public Advertiser. March 18, April 7, and May 12, 1819.

A German in Missouri—1829

Christensen, Lawrence, et al. *Dictionary of Missouri Biography.* Columbia: University of Missouri Press, 1999.

Duden, Gottfried. *Report on a Journey to the Western States of North America.* James Goodrich, general editor. Columbia: State Historical Society of Missouri and University of Missouri Press, 1980.

McCandless, Perry. *A History of Missouri. Volume II: 1820 to 1860.* Columbia: University of Missouri Press, 1972.

A Slave Sues for His Freedom—1846–1856

Finkelman, Paul. *Dred Scott vs. Sandford: A Brief History with Documents.* Boston: Bedford Books, 1997.

Greene, Lorenzo J., et al. *Missouri's Black Heritage.* St. Louis: Forum Press, 1980.

McCandless, Perry. *A History of Missouri. Volume II: 1820 to 1860.* Columbia: University of Missouri Press, 1972.

Merkel, Benjamin. "The Abolition Aspects of Missouri's Antislavery Controversy, 1819–1865." *Missouri Historical Review* 44, no. 3 (April 1950).

The Saluda Disaster—1852

Day, Elder, and Sister Robert O. *The Steamboat* Saluda *Disaster: An Overview.* Salt Lake City: Church of Jesus Christ of Latter-day Saints, April 1992.

Hartley, William, and Fred Woods. "Explosion of the Steamboat *Saluda:* Tragedy and Compassion at Lexington, Missouri, 1852." *Missouri Historical Review* 99, no. 4 (July 2005).

McCandless, Perry. *A History of Missouri. Volume II: 1820 to 1860.* Columbia: University of Missouri Press, 1972.

The Pony Express Sets Out—1860

Di Certo, Joseph J. *The Saga of the Pony Express.* Missoula, Mont.: Mountain Press Publishing Company, 2003.

Hagen, Olaf, "The Pony Express Starts from St. Joseph." *Missouri Historical Review* 43, no. 1 (October 1948).

McCandless, Perry. *A History of Missouri. Volume II: 1820 to 1860.* Columbia: University of Missouri Press, 1972.

The Weekly West. April 7, 1860.

Welsh, Donald H. "The Pony Express in Retrospect." *Missouri Historical Review* 54, no. 3 (April 1960).

The First Civil War Shots in Missouri—1861

Castel, Albert. *General Sterling Price and the Civil War in the West.* Baton Rouge: Louisiana State University Press, 1968.

Gerteis, Louis. *Civil War St. Louis.* Lawrence: University Press of Kansas, 2001.

Monaghan, Jay. *Civil War on the Western Border, 1854–1865.* New York: Bonanza Books, 1960.

Parrish, William. *A History of Missouri. Volume III: 1860 to 1875.* Columbia: University of Missouri Press, 1973.

Black Troops Show Their Mettle—1862

Brownlee, Richard S. *Gray Ghosts of the Confederacy: Guerilla Warfare in the West, 1861–1865.* Baton Rouge: Louisiana State University Press, 1984.

Greene, Lorenzo J., et al. *Missouri's Black Heritage.* St. Louis: Forum Press, 1980.

Monaghan, Jay. *Civil War on the Western Border 1854–1865.* New York: Bonanza Books, 1960.

New York Times. August 20, 1862.

General Price's Invasion of Missouri—1864

Bartels, Carolyn. *The Last Long Mile: Westport to Arkansas, October 1864*. Independence, Mo.: Two Trails Publishing, 1999.

Brownlee, Richard S. *Gray Ghosts of the Confederacy: Guerilla Warfare in the West, 1861–1865*. Baton Rouge: Louisiana State University Press, 1984.

Gerteis, Louis. *Civil War St. Louis*. Lawrence: University Press of Kansas, 2001.

Monaghan, Jay. *Civil War on the Western Border, 1854–1865*. New York: Bonanza Books, 1960.

Parrish, William. *A History of Missouri. Volume III: 1860 to 1875*. Columbia: University of Missouri Press, 1973.

Outlaws, Lawmen, and Outlaw Lawmen—1872

Draper, William R., and Mabel Draper. *Old Grubstake Days in Joplin*. Girard, Kans.: Haldeman-Julius Publications, 1946.

Hounschell, Jim. *Lawmen and Outlaws: 116 Years in Joplin's History*. Joplin, Mo.: Walsworth Publishing, 1989.

Renner, G. K. *Joplin: From Mining Town to Urban Center*. Northridge, Calif.: Windsor Publications, 1985.

Shaner, Dolph. *The Story of Joplin*. New York: Stratford House, 1948.

The James Gang Robs a Train—1874

Beights, Ronald. *Jesse James and the First Missouri Train Robbery*. Gretna, La.: Pelican Publishing, 2002.

Brownlee, Richard S. *Gray Ghosts of the Confederacy: Guerilla Warfare in the West, 1861–1865*. Baton Rouge: Louisiana State University Press, 1984.

Christensen, Lawrence, et al. *Dictionary of Missouri Biography.* Columbia: University of Missouri Press, 1999.

St. Louis Dispatch. February 5, 1874.

St. Louis Republican. October 6, 1882.

Settle, William A. *Jesse James Was His Name.* Columbia: University of Missouri Press, 1966.

Connecting the Bootheel to the World—1880

Christensen, Lawrence, and Gary Kremer. *A History of Missouri. Volume IV: 1875 to 1919.* Columbia: University of Missouri Press, 2004.

Doherty, William. *Louis Houck: Missouri Historian and Entrepreneur.* Columbia: University of Missouri Press, 1961.

Rhodes, Joel. "The Father of Southeast Missouri: Louis Houck and the Coming of the Railroad." *Missouri Historical Review* 100, no. 2 (January 2006).

Champion Cyclists Race in Clarksville—1887

Anonymous, "The Clarksville Road Race." *The Wheel* no. 287 (April 1, 1887).

Caldwell, Dorothy J. "Cyclists Raced for World Championship at Clarksville in 1887." *Missouri Historical Review* 58, no. 3 (April 1964).

St. Louis Post-Dispatch, May 24–25, 1887.

The "Kansas Cyclone" Descends on Missouri—1901

Caldwell, Dorothy J. "Carry Nation, a Missouri Woman, Won Fame in Kansas." *Missouri Historical Review* 63, no. 4 (July 1969).

Christensen, Lawrence, and Gary Kremer. *A History of Missouri. Volume IV: 1875 to 1919.* Columbia: University of Missouri Press, 2004.

Grace, Fran. *Carry A. Nation: Retelling the Life.* Indianapolis: Indiana University Press, 2001.

Kansas City Star. April 15, 1901.

St. Louis Post-Dispatch. March 25, 1901.

Taylor, Robert Lewis. *Vessel of Wrath: The Life and Times of Carry Nation.* New York: New American Library, 1966.

The Toughest Marathon in History—1904

Christensen, Lawrence, and Gary Kremer. *A History of Missouri. Volume IV: 1875 to 1919.* Columbia: University of Missouri Press, 2004.

Lucas, Charles. *The Olympic Games: 1904.* St. Louis: Woodward & Tiernan Printing, 1905.

Matthews, George, and Sandra Marshall. *St. Louis Olympics 1904.* Chicago: Arcadia Publishing, 2003.

Joseph Folk Cleans Up Missouri—1905

Christensen, Lawrence, and Gary Kremer. *A History of Missouri. Volume IV: 1875 to 1919.* Columbia: University of Missouri Press, 2004.

Parrish, William, Charles Jones Jr., and Lawrence Christensen. *Missouri: The Heart of the Nation.* 3rd ed. Wheeling, Ill.: Harlan Davidson, 2004.

Piott, Steven. *Holy Joe: Joseph W. Folk and the Missouri Idea.* Columbia: University of Missouri Press, 1997.

Winn, Kenneth. "It All Adds Up: Reform and the Erosion of Representative Government in Missouri, 1900–2000." *Official*

Manual of the State of Missouri, 1999–2000. Jefferson City, Mo.: Secretary of State, 2000.

Fire at the Capital!—1911

Christensen, Lawrence, and Gary Kremer. *A History of Missouri. Volume IV: 1875 to 1919.* Columbia: University of Missouri Press, 2004.

Parrish, William, Charles Jones Jr., and Lawrence Christensen. *Missouri: The Heart of the Nation.* 3rd ed. Wheeling, Ill.: Harlan Davidson, 2004.

Summers, Joseph S., Jr. *The Day the Capitol Burned.* Jefferson City, Mo.: CeMoMedServ Publications, 1986.

The Golden Lane—1916

Dains, Mary, ed. *Show Me Missouri Women: Selected Biographies.* Kirksville, Mo.: Thomas Jefferson University Press, 1989.

Laas, Virginia Jeans, ed. *Bridging Two Eras: The Autobiography of Emily Newell Blair, 1877–1951.* Columbia: University of Missouri Press, 1999.

McMillen, Margot Ford, and Heather Roberson. *Into the Spotlight: Four Missouri Women.* Columbia: University of Missouri Press, 2004.

St. Louis Post-Dispatch. June 12, 1916.

Springfield and the Great Streetcar Strike—1916

Fink, Gary. *Labor's Search for Political Order.* Columbia: University of Missouri Press, 1973.

McIntyre, Stephen. "'The City Belongs to the Local Unions': The Rise of the Springfield Labor Movement, 1871–1912." *Missouri Historical Review* 98, no. 1 (October 2003).

Robison, Elijah. *The Streetcar Strike of 1916–17: "Scabs, Conspiracy, and Lawlessness in Springfield, Missouri."* Springfield, Mo.: Greene County Archives Bulletin Number Sixty-Seven, 2004.

Springfield Republican. February 19, 1916–June 16, 1917.

Luella St. Clair Moss Runs for Congress—1922

Boonville Advertiser. July 20–21, 1922.

Christensen, Lawrence, et al. *Dictionary of Missouri Biography.* Columbia: University of Missouri Press, 1999.

Columbia Daily Tribune. July 7, August 1–2, 1922.

Dains, Mary. "The Congressional Campaign of Luella St. Clair Moss." *Missouri Historical Review* 82, no. 4 (July 1988).

Dains, Mary, ed. *Show Me Missouri Women: Selected Biographies.* Kirksville, Mo.: Thomas Jefferson University Press, 1989.

Moniteau County Herald. June 1, 1922.

St. Louis Post-Dispatch. October 15, August 13, 1922.

The Cardinals' First World Series—1926

Christensen, Lawrence, et al. *Dictionary of Missouri Biography.* Columbia: University of Missouri Press, 1999.

Kirkendall, Richard. *A History of Missouri. Volume V: 1919 to 1953.* Columbia: University of Missouri Press, 1986.

McLear, Patrick. "'Gentlemen, Reach for All': Toppling the Pendergast Machine, 1936–1940." *Missouri Historical Review* 95, no. 1 (October 2000).

Reddig, William. *Tom's Town: Kansas City and the Pendergast Legend.* Columbia: University of Missouri Press, 1986.

BIBLIOGRAPHY

Breaking the Pendergast Machine—1939

Durant, John. *Highlights of the World Series.* New York: Hastings House Publishers, 1971.

St. Louis Post-Dispatch. October 11, 1926.

Smith, Robert. *World Series: The Games and Players.* Garden City, NY: Doubleday, 1967.

From Missouri to the White House—1948

Christensen, Lawrence, et al. *Dictionary of Missouri Biography.* Columbia: University of Missouri Press, 1999.

Kirkendall, Richard. *A History of Missouri. Volume V: 1919 to 1953.* Columbia: University of Missouri Press, 1986.

Misse, Fred. "Truman, Berlin, and the 1948 Election." *Missouri Historical Review* 76, no. 2 (January 1982).

Neal, Steve, ed. *Miracle of '48.* Carbondale: Southern Illinois University Press, 2003.

Jesse James is Alive!—1949

Steele, Phillip W., and George Warfel. *The Many Faces of Jesse James.* Gretna, La.: Pelican Publishing Company, 1995.

Wood, Joe. *My Jesse James Story.* Washington, Mo.: The Missourian Publishing Company, Inc., 1989.

Yeatman, Ted P. *Frank and Jesse James: The Story Behind the Legend.* Nashville, Tenn.: Cumberland House, 2000.

Building the Arch—1965

Jordan, Paul, and Bruce Dale. "New Spirit Soars in Mid-America's Proud Old City." *National Geographic,* November 1965.

Larsen, Lawrence. *A History of Missouri. Volume VI: 1953 to 2003.* Columbia: University of Missouri Press, 2004.

Mehrhoff, W. Arthur. *The Gateway Arch: Fact and Symbol.* Bowling Green, Ohio: Bowling Green State University Popular Press, 1992.

St. Louis Globe-Democrat. October 29, 1965.

St. Louis Post-Dispatch. January 19, 1958.

Missouri: The Flood State—1993

Burnett, Betty, ed. *The Flood of 1993: Stories from a Midwestern Disaster.* Tucson: Patrice Press, 1994.

Hurley, J., and Roberta Hagood. *Hannibal Courier-Post Edition of Hannibal Flood '93.* Hannibal, Mo.: Hannibal Courier-Post, 1994.

Larsen, Lawrence. *A History of Missouri. Volume VI: 1953 to 2003.* Columbia: University of Missouri Press, 2004.

Missouri Facts & Trivia

Fisher, John C. *Catfish, Fiddles, Mules, and More: Missouri's State Symbols.* Columbia: University of Missouri Press, 2003.

Young, Josh. *Missouri Curiosities.* Guilford, Conn.: Globe Pequot Press, 2003.

INDEX

INDEX

ABOUT THE AUTHOR

Sean McLachlan first came to Missouri in the early 1990s to earn a master's degree in archaeology at the University of Missouri–Columbia and fell in love with the rich heritage of the state. He worked for ten years as an archaeologist in Israel, Cyprus, Bulgaria, and various places in the United States before enrolling in the University of Missouri's School of Journalism, where he earned a second master's degree. Now a full-time writer, his writings have appeared in such publications as *Missouri Life, British Heritage,* and *Ancient Egypt.* He is the author of numerous books including the novel *A Fine Likeness* set in Civil War Missouri. Visit him on the web at civilwarhorror.blogspot.com.